MW00989386

3/23/2003

Digital Storytellers

The Art of Communicating the Gospel in Worship

Len Wilson and Jason Moore

Abingdon Press

DIGITAL STORYTELLERS
THE ART OF COMMUNICATING THE GOSPEL IN WORSHIP

© Copyright 2002 by Len Wilson and Jason Moore

All rights reserved.

Unless otherwise noted, video clips on the bundled DVD, which are all created by the authors, are used by permission of UMR Communications.

Unless otherwise noted, Scripture references are from the New Revised Standard Version of the Bible, © 1989 by the National Council of Churches in Christ. Used by permission.

Scripture references marked (NIV) are from the New Internation Version of the Bible, copyright 1973, 1978, and 1984 by International Bible Society.

Library of Congress Cataloging in Publication is available.

Printing: 1

To discuss this book with the author and others, please go to www.Abingdon.com/ebooks.

Acknowledgments

There are many people who have supported one or both of us during the creation of *Digital Storytellers*. Our editor, Paul Franklyn, is an incredible blessing. We are equally thankful for his editorial skills and his passion for this subject matter.

Many past and present colleagues in ministry have given us seeds, scrutiny, and support. We are thankful for the handful of courageous people who have dared with us to dream Lumicon Digital Productions. UMR Communications CEO Ron Patterson, along with Tom Boomershine, Amelia Cooper, and Richard Beaty, joined with us in attempting something much larger than possible in starting this venture. Ericka Robinson and Michael Clements helped nurture the dream of Lumicon since, as we all together witnessed God's movement.

Mike Slaughter and the members of the worship design team at Ginghamsburg Church provided a laboratory for these ideas, before we left to pursue Lumicon, for which we are very grateful. We give special thanks to Ginghamsburg Global for permission to use some of our previous work.

Thanks is deserved by digital age pastors from all over the country, who encourage us professionally and personally. Without them we have no work to do.

Colleagues in digital age ministry, such as Todd Carter, Bill Easum, Tim Eason, and the staff at *Technologies for Worship* magazine allowed us to test much of the material in this book. We are grateful to Jeff and Debra Friend for continued advice and counsel, and special thanks goes to Jeff Friend for making our productions sound better.

Jason: In early 2000 I sat in a production suite with Len Wilson and began to discuss how we might help church leaders move ahead into the digital age. That conversation began this book. At the time I wanted to write a book about how to help artists quench their creative thirst in congregational ministry. Our ideas intertwined so much that Len's *Digital Storytellers* is now woven together with my dreams for *The Art of Communicating the Gospel in Worship*.

I have always wanted to be an artist. I lived out this passion in my life through drawing, music, acting, writing, and working full-time in a church ministry. Through each of these experiences my parents stood with me in every way they could. Bob Moore, my father, is my hero and a guiding light in my development as a person. He taught me perspective, both in art and in life. My mother, Karen Moore, loves unconditionally. She is my biggest and most supportive fan in all of my endeavors. I am grateful to my sister Julie and brother Justin for continually sharing their support for me and the things I do. My extended family graciously support me after uprooting to Texas, a land far away from Ohio.

Thanks to Lee Strawhun for showing me Jesus. You showed me that my artistic gifts could be used for God's glory and your passion for ministry ignited God's calling in my life. Mark Quinter helped me believe in myself. Larry Butt challenged me both in life and in ministry. Thanks to Kasey Hitt, for your friendship and help with exploring various concepts in this book. Thanks to to Jeff and Ingrid Turcotte for your friendship and continued support.

Many thanks to Grace United Methodist Church in Piqua, Ohio, for nurturing me through youth: specifically, Ace and Jo Justice, and Kirby and Jana Warren, provided me with second homes to grow in Christ. Thanks to Mike Lyons, who hired me at Ginghamsburg. You took a chance on me despite my lack of experience.

Never-ending thanks belong to my beautiful wife, Michele, who has always been a major support to me in my most stressed times. Thank you for understanding when I am busy doing fifty million things. You have brought much joy to what, without you, would be a very lonely life.

Len: As is the case for many authors, this book started the week after my first book, *The Wired Church*, was completed. Over the three years that followed, my growing collection of Post-its, torn envelopes, and scribbled sheets of notes became increasingly intertwined with the ideas and work of my close personal friend and colleague in ministry, Jason Moore. People tell us when we speak together that as much or more than what we have to say, they appreciate the way we finish each other's sentences.

Thanks to my family as they continue to support my passion. My wife and best friend, Shar Leigh Wilson, rides the roller coaster of my life with all smiles and love. My sister, Lori Fast, my mother, Marylin Dickerson, and my father, Wayne Wilson, have each been valuable critics and sounding boards for the ideas in the pages to follow. Also, a special thank you to Bobby and Sally Soefje for their apparently unwavering belief that I'm a great husband for their daughter.

And last, a public thank-you to God for giving Shar and I a newborn child that I am sure has DNA more digital than I can possibly know. I dedicate *Digital Storytellers* to my daughter, Kaylyn Love Wilson.

CONTENTS

Foreword

You're standing in the center of one of the great European cathedrals prior to the first world war. Immediately, your eyes are drawn to the large stain glass panels surrounding the seating area. Captivated by their beauty and simplicity, you follow the biblical story from panel to panel. Time after time, your eyes sweep around the cathedral, each time absorbing the story faster and faster until finally the static, stain glass images begin to take on a life of their own. Suddenly, for the first time in your life, you *experience* the story instead of just reading or hearing about the story. You've just experienced the Gospel in a primitive form of digital media and your life will never be the same.

Most of us know we are living in an emerging world that will be much different than the one in which we were born. Everything is changing, including the way we must communicate our faith to be effective. In our book, *Growing Spiritual Redwoods*, Tom Bandy and I remind the reader, *"If you say it all with words, you have missed the point."*

A whole new digital world is emerging today. Can you see it? If you can, you know it is a world built on emotional, virtual, holographic, decentralized, holistic, empowered, one-to-one, borderless, bottom-up, global/local, and egalitarian characteristics. Such a world will play by totally different rules than the rules of modernity. In the twenty-first century to *not be digital* will be the new form of illiteracy

Throughout recorded history, the forward movement of Christianity has mostly been in direct proportion to way Christian explorers have handled the convergence of Spirit and technology. Three such convergences have occurred in the history of Christianity: The Roman Road, the printing press, and now the digital age. Paul and the Christian missionaries used the Roman roads to spread the Good News. Martin Luther and the Reformers used the printing press. Who will be the digital storytellers of our time?

Len and Jason will challenge *you* to become a digital storyteller. They will take you beyond simply flashing words on a screen, or using story to communicate the truth, or even using a screen. They will take you beyond these pieces of technology to the "interface" of worship and technology so that the mechanics of the production of worship disappear and, like reading a book, we reach the point where we no longer see the technology, for it has become a part of our life. To become digital storytellers means that some of you must allow God to totally rewire the way we feel, think, and communicate.

Get ready for a digital mindshift!

Bill Easum
www.easumbandy.com

Chapter 1
Convergence

Len: My wife and I are pregnant. One of the first things we decided to do when we heard the news was to buy matching cell phones so we could stay in contact with each other all the time. As with all purchases of things I don't understand, for a month I research on cellular plans on the web, at malls, and in the newspaper. After my extensive investigation, however, I ended up more confused than I had been before I started. I encountered the same confusion in trying to get the best configuration of cable television and high-speed Internet at my home: Do I go with traditional coaxial cable runs, miniature satellite dishes, expanded service from the local Bell, or some combination? New technology is thoroughly difficult. I can't wait until access to technology no longer means paying invoices for multiple different services, each with its own provider. Cell phones are becoming PDAs, laptops are becoming televisions, movies are on the Internet, and everything is coming together to a by now clichéd point called "convergence."

Convergence is a buzzword that gained currency through the 1990s as technology industry insiders envisioned empires in which their respective devices merge. But more than just a business trend for the new millennium, the hype over convergence is symbolic of the adolescence of the digital age. The present world of desktop computing, which is called "the second wave"(mainframes were the first), will eventually converge into a third wave, called "ubiquitous computing,"[1] where our reclining easy chair will tell our phone not to accept calls and our pressed-on pillow can turn off our nightstand light. It's like "the Clapper," where everything is powered by microchips that we won't even see or notice.

Even though the introduction of new digital technologies seems to be occurring at breakneck speed, most new digital products are only minor steps in the continuing trend toward this third wave. The overall process of the birth of a digital culture is taking generations.

The rise of digital culture

Historically, advancements in technology take a long time to broadly affect culture. For example, though the Israelites had historically worshiped God in oral culture, the early Church operated within a changing communication construct marked by a symbolic climax in John's words, which found legitimacy in their audience because they were written and not spoken (John 20:31). The assimilation of manuscript communication in ancient Roman culture took generations as well. The maturation of the printing press took generations, too, from its birth in the mid-fifteenth century to the day Martin Luther posted his "95 Theses" on the Wittenberg door, which is now regarded by the compartmental forces of history to be the watershed to a mass print culture for the Church.

Similarly, the twentieth century was about the gestation, birth, and development of a new era, with its own particular communication system. Different people cite different birth dates, from 1896's film to 1927's film with sound to the 1949–1950 TV "revolution" to 1962's color TV "revolution" to 1968's social "revolution." Historians will clarify these discussions. What matters is that we are now a few generations into a new culture, and the watershed moment, somewhere across our postmodern landscape, has already occurred. The digital deconstruction has been happening for years now, and only the most unplugged churches are unaware of the upheaval.

In each era the church has been forced to acknowledge and respond to massive changes in communication technology. The comfortable response is usually for churches to retreat to established forms of Gospel communication from an earlier era, where problems in interpretation have mostly been worked out. Peter argued with early Church leaders in Acts 15 that Gentiles should not be forced to accept the culture, norms, and communication style of the established religion of Judaism. Centuries later, the Catholic Church first attempted widespread use of the printing press as a way to reinforce norms through the publication of scripts containing the "correct" Latin Mass, which was then distributed to distant outpost parishes that had been adapting the Mass in form and language to make it understandable to its indigenous communities. In each era forces of change eventually swept away those who wanted to avoid the hard work of reinterpreting the Gospel for new generations.

The pattern is repeated today. The twentieth-century church imitated the fifteenth-century church, by using radio, television, and other emerging digital age media to reinforce "traditional" (read: modern-era) worship. But the forces of change are beginning to overwhelm those who wish to maintain the status quo. One study in the secular audiovisual industry asserts that over 75 percent of churches in North America have purchased or are planning to purchase technology systems in the coming year. The typical system costs around $10,000 and consists of a screen, a projector, a computer, and a videocassette and/or DVD player. A randomized telephone study of 364 churches by our publisher shows that 38 percent of congregations are projecting media at this time (using front, rear, and older overhead projectors) and that an additional 20 percent of churches plan to do so within the next year. Sixty-two percent of the users have the capability to handle graphic projection, and 94 percent are projecting song lyrics (using PowerPoint 75 percent of the time, or transparencies for 17 percent of the users). This trend is the objective of our earlier book, *The Wired Church: Making Media Ministry.*

The Wired Church attempts to outline a series of strategies for churches to begin to use media in their church life, including design, team building, and technical alternatives. The most important advice, however, fostered understanding about how to create media that communicates to digital culture. The first goal is to get a congregation to accept technology as an integral part of church life. Since writing *The Wired Church*, I now know that my original purpose—to speak the Gospel in the language of the culture—is not enough, because churches *say* they will use technology and *claim* that technology is the cultural language, but still not "get it." Many church leaders do not yet have an idea of how digital media are capable of empowering churches to transform lives with the Gospel of Jesus. Further, many congregations lack a strategy and only purchase technology for worship and/or education out of a vague awareness of a hot trend. Churches point to success stories in their own regions and national stories like Ginghamsburg Church, whose worship attendance tripled from 1,000 to 3,000 in three years with the introduction of teams and media in worship, as both inspiration for their own digital media strategies and as frustration ("works for large churches but not mine") when it is not happening to their congregation in the same way.

The typical church media story

There is a common story emerging as churches seek to stay current during this period of great change. Typically, somebody says in a leadership meeting (often it is the senior pastor or the worship leader), "We need to get a screen."

To be more relevant with the needs of our current congregation	92%
To be more culturally relevant	89%
To attract and keep the youth in our congregation	85%
To attract the unchurched to our worship services	84%
To motivate a group of volunteers who have media or computer technology skills	33%
To respond to changes in worship at other nearby congregations	32%
To save money on the purchase of printed worship resources	12%
To be different from other churches	9%
Get heads out of books/look up	4%
Other	12%

From an Abingdon Press study of 364 congregations

They might say, "Lyrics on the screen are better than reading them from the hymnbook," or "We need to reach the young people in the community." So they do that, and over the objections of many and through theological, political, and economic battles, the church leadership gets their equipment installed. This breakthrough takes six months to years, depending on the tenacity of the change agent(s).

The transition causes uproar and makes worship interesting for a while, sometimes in an intrusive sort of way. Technology lovers within the church volunteer and are recruited to operate the equipment, and eventually worship settles into a pattern of using lyrics, sermon points, and an occasional movie clip on the screen.

In spite of all their vision and implementation, many churches find that no long-term substantial difference occurs in the content or attributes of their worship communication. After twelve to twenty-four months the worship planners may become aware that the presence of digital technology alone has little impact on producing authentic, indigenous digital age worship. They begin to suggest, "We need to go to the next level," or "We've got to raise the standards of excellence," or "We need to become more contemporary." Regardless of the language, there is behind these attitudes a desire to share good news and grow disciples of Jesus. There is an awareness that digital media, as it is being offered, is not contributing substantially to that mission. In fact, some church leaders, out of frustration, even develop theological rationale for why it is neither appropriate nor possible for digital media to communicate the Word of God in the same way that established forms of oral and written media have succeeded.[2]

In Chapter 3, we will look into these errant theologies, which understand "media as servant." But the most immediate problem, and the founding purpose of this project, is to throw away the dominant construct of "presentation" media, as it is commonly known in the business world. This construct, known as "multi-media" (with or without the hyphen), is rooted in early 1990s PC development. At the time, vision for digital technology surpassed reality, and most computers had limited capability for sound or video. To participate in "multi-media," at most, meant to create a presentation in a software application like Microsoft PowerPoint and Adobe Persuasion, built over a color gradient background, with clip art, bullet points, and postage stamp–size video clips inserted at various points. An entire industry sprang up around the "postage stamp" media approach. Much of streaming video on web sites is based on thumbnail projection, due to bandwidth limits. Business trades developed for how to make the perfect postage–stamp video presentations.

Now, a decade later, PCs are much more powerful, and sound and video have become standard computer components, but the outdated model that led these technical developments still stands. Improvements in technology have not led to an advanced style but rather a faster, flashier version of the older style, with bullet points that fly and twist and bigger postage stamp boxes for video. Even full-size video will sometimes break up the same representative gradient color backgrounds. Because of this trend, the term *multimedia* has come to symbolize a business-driven, computer-based standard that consists of a number of textual, aural, and visual elements tossed together in a PowerPoint document, with little sense of design and zero sense of story or experience. PowerPoint is most frequently a medium that is neither rare nor well done.

Jason: We were talking with one of the members of our team about her experience with PowerPoint. She admits that it is addictive to play with all the toys within the program when creating a presentation. The simple ability to make text fly around in PowerPoint is fun for her. She also commented that it is very simple to use and is self-contained.

I understand the appeal of playing with the various bells and whistles inside a computer application. The first time I opened the 3-D application I now use regularly, I found a tool that automatically created a banana. I immediately tried it out, and really impressed myself as an artist: I made a banana! Eventually I learned that I have no need for a banana in any of the animations I've created. Once I saw how the application could be used, I forgot about the toys and focused on using the program to create art. I don't dismiss PowerPoint; in fact I use it every time I present. I merely think it is misused as an end in itself.

I attended one church that was trying hard but was stuck in a corporate presentation mode. They are a typical PowerPoint church. Every other sentence that left the pastor's mouth became an animated point via PowerPoint on the screen. Text flying in circles, shooting in from the left, falling from the top, and "OH MY! . . . She can't take much more, Captain Kirk!" That kind of sensory overload made keeping up with the pastor feel like running on a treadmill that is stuck on the high rotation. Cheesy clip-art filled the screen on several occasions, and the graphics for the most part were solid backgrounds or gradients. The experience left me feeling flat. If only they had used a present-day metaphor, a film clip that related in some way to my life, or an artistic image that communicated to me at a heart or soul level—in the same way that icons functioned for preliterate Christians—I might have been sent forth inspired and excited by the message.

Why is this business model so prevalent? The media solution for most churches is usually to seek out someone from the congregation who might be considered the "techno geek," or use the church secretary, or find some-one who has experience building business presentations.

"We have PowerPoint." Most folks think this means that they "have arrived," and many stop there. Digital media is capable of so much more.

Many of these "PowerPointers" are making an attempt, but they simply have never experienced a model other than what is offered in boardrooms.

New media, old mind-sets

The problem is most churches are still rooted in "informa-tion" as the purpose for communication. Although many con-gregations that are trying to reach the digital culture start by adding a screen in worship, it is used as an expensive hymnal replacement. Some churches use both hymnals and screens, so basically they're repeating text on the screen that is available in print form in the pew in front of them. Some of those same churches are using the screen as a giant bulletin board to share the weekly announcements. Sometimes announcements (if presented with narrative tensions) can be transformational, but if the screen is like an information kiosk, it's probably a misuse of church resources.

Even with some of the more advanced churches that are starting to create original video, most of them are very informational in their approach. "On-the-street" videos are a great way to start for churches beginning to use media equipment, but they are not usually based in story. In a sense, "on-the-street" videos are just another way of gathering and then presenting information. I don't dislike them (in fact we produce them all the time), but I think that churches can become complacent with the format. Even mission videos can become information reports, rather than a story that can touch the heart of worshipers. **(For an example of an on-the-street video, experience "StreetTalk: What Do You Hope For?" Chapter 03 on the DVD.)**

L: The root fallacy of the business presentation model in worship is that it ignores both a fundamental part of digital culture and a fundamental part of authentic worship. Throughout the modern age, the church became very good at crunching data. Too much so, if you believe as I do that denominations are often a product of too much *debate over doctrinal minutia*. The church needs to awaken to a culture that leaves modernism behind. Ironically, although we live in the "Information Age," people don't want or need more information, be it preached or formed into flying bullet points. The church wants to use digital technology to crunch its data faster and better, but what people crave is an experience of God.

J: When I was choosing a career path, I decided that I was going to be a commercial artist. A friend of mine who was also an artist had decided that she was going to take the "fine arts" path. There was often tension between us because she thought that selling one's artwork was selling one's soul, and she was also against using computers to create art. To her and many fine artists, the term "digital art" is an oxy-moron. I guess she felt that the most pure forms of art were created with more traditional, primitive materials.

My friend is not alone in her mind-set. Many fine artists share her attitudes toward commercial art and using digital technology to create art in general. Although tension remains strong, a shift is under way.

In March of 2000 Len and I were speaking in Chicago. During our time there we took several walks through the city. On one of these walks we came across a large art store that sold supplies. One of the windows had a small sign that read: "We sell computer art supplies." I was astonished! We went into the store and I asked the sales person if they sold many computer art supplies. He reluc-tantly said that they were starting to sell more and more. Digital art is beginning to gain acceptance in many circles that once dismissed it.

On the Internet I discover sites featuring digitally pro-duced art created specifically as "fine art." Artists, both commercial and fine, realize that digital technology is merely a set of different tools to create high-quality, contem-plative art. The possibilities are endless for what can be cre-ated with these new tools. Harnessing this technology will allow Christians to share the Gospel in new and more pow-erful ways, and it will allow us to create worship that will allow people to see God in ways that they never have before.

The church must make the jump from modern formulas for ministry to the postmodern, or more accurately digital, forms if it expects to reach the culture of the digital age. Worship can and will become rooted in digital culture forms but continue to reinvigorate the traditions that have come before us. This transition in digital culture is based upon experience, rather than meaning.

While on my honeymoon in Orlando, I saw a form of experiential marketing that reaches out to digital culture. My wife, Michele, and I were walking through the Down-town Disney area when we decided to stop for a bite to eat. After several days of eating expensive theme park food, we thought McDonald's would be quick and easy on the budget.

Michele and I were standing in line when all of a sudden the menu caught my eye. The menus in this particular McDonald's were all flat-screen video monitors. Part of the time they displayed prices, and had the look of the menus you see in most McDonald's. Otherwise they were displaying various menu items. The items weren't static; they were moving video. Salads were tossed, steam billowed from coffee, and various McCreations were prepared. This actually, for a brief moment, made me change the way I perceived fast food. Those screens made what typically looks like a doctored photo come to life. The presentation made that food look so good that I almost ordered a Grilled Chicken (even though I'm allergic to chicken!).

Something about seeing the sights and sounds presented on those flat screens gave me an experience that made me forget all that I had seen during two years of labor under the golden arches, and made me actually eagerly anticipate tasting my value meal. The culture of the digital age craves experience, and future generations of believers are children of the digital culture.

L: This craving is causing great upheaval in structures and institutions such as the Church that are married to the modern era and its emphasis on analysis. In this period of great transition, a long-silent group in the Church is once again finding voice. This group understands that technology and culture, though related, are different things, and has been using technology for entirely different cultural expressions. While incorporating the best of belief–system formation in the modern era, these expressions don't simply analyze faith, but acknowledge and celebrate the mystery of the presence of God. As the digital age forms, this group is picking up the remains of an ancient tradition and all of its mutated forms. This tradition is story. These storytellers, who were once celebrated by the Church, are once again being empowered with multiple communication systems at their disposal. Their new title is Producer, and they work best with other like-minded people. The Church desperately needs them. This breed of digital artist will be capable of producing great quality individually, but even greater works within a team. Their collective teams will form the preaching tradition for the twenty-first century, because they are masters of multiple communication forms that put their skills to use by telling the stories of our shared faith.

J: We believe that the future of media in church will only thrive if advocates begin to use an artistic, narrative approach as they design worship. This means that the screen is used to communicate thoughts, ideas, and feelings that can touch people at a much deeper level. Projected song lyrics and sermon points alone cannot meet the need.

L: In the chapters that follow, our purpose is not to provide a comprehensive reading on any of the subjects of postmodernism, popular culture, digital technology, art, or innovations in ministry. Rather, this project is about the convergence of these disparate subjects into the emerging architecture of digital age worship. We will explain from experience about how to deal with the ministry fallout from this radical sociological shift (which has impact on religious authority), and, most important, how becoming a digital storyteller will transform your communication of the Gospel. But first, in order to fully understand and produce digital media that relates to the ancient traditions of worship but is communicated to our digital culture, it is important to outline the nature of digital culture.

1. Paul Wallich, "Practical Magic," in *Discover* (December 2000), pp. 48-49.
2. Some of these critics include Marva Dawn, Neil Postman, and William Fore.

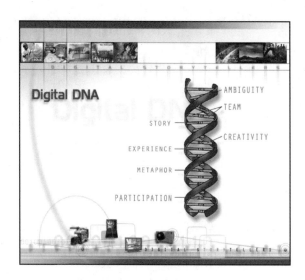

Chapter 2
Digital DNA

J: A pastor came toward us at a speaking engagement with the strong need to "go digital" in order to reach people in his community. He decided to start immediately by signing up for a subscription to our services. One of our team members walked him through our web site, which is our primary delivery system for the subscription. He listened intently to her explanation but, in trying to follow, he became confused, then frustrated.

He then made a statement that was very telling about his predicament: "I want so badly to reach this generation, but I'm just an old dinosaur who wants to go digital. I just don't understand this like you young people." What is this mysterious ingredient that young adults carry around? We call it Digital DNA.

L: At another speaking engagement a gentleman (solidly "Gen X") approached me. He is an ordained United Methodist, and he wears a priest's collar. He was on the verge of weeping as he spoke to me, as he explained his desperation in trying to learn how to create digital age worship. He said to me, "I'm thirty-three and I feel like I'm two generations away from people my own age!" I got the impression as we talked that he felt that he had sold his identity to a literate, modernist paradigm for ministry, perhaps out of ignorance, weakness, or the desire to advance himself professionally, and he is now desperately seeking a postmodern strategy to restore his original passions for following Jesus into the mission field.

As we spoke it occurred to me that my friends and acquaintances in ministry, at least younger than age thirty-five, are in some way participating in redefining worship for a digital culture. (Older leaders from the boomer generation began the shift in terms of music for worship.) I'm not sure this is an insurgency as much as it is an expression of identity. Even for those of my peers who couldn't say that they are intentionally conducting ministry according to a particular epistemological paradigm, they are apparently acting out of what they know innately to be true.

J: I can relate to this search for identity. While in school I was an active participant and leader in the youth ministry known as YoungLife. The area director in charge of our school, Larry Butt, encouraged some of us to create sketches for our weekly events. We decided as a way to make YoungLife more attractive for everyone that we would create a weekly video. We produced a serial comedy sketch that entertained, and (usually) communicated the Gospel to the thirty or forty youths who attended on a regular basis. The video serial was called "Marvelous Martha," and although it had a weak plot, it was basically a vehicle for a series of wacky stunts. The first part of the sketch was a live performance to set up a subsequent "live" video of our characters performing some sort of impossible stunt. After the clips, Larry or another speaker would refer to the characters and then relate them to the Gospel message of the week.

Within a few weeks of debuting the "Marvelous Martha" series, buzz spread throughout our school. Many students in the halls and cafeteria began asking what would happen next. We were unprepared for the response. The houses where we met were filled to capacity. Standing room only crowds formed in the back of the room. During the school year YoungLife grew from about 30 to more than 150 persons, because the youth were attracted to the Gospel message through a culturally appealing methodology.

In retrospect, I realize that we had no detailed three-step mission plan on how and why we used media to speak the Gospel each week at YoungLife meetings. Without a clue as to why we were engaging the culture with video and drama, we knew that the youth loved this stuff, and that it made all the difference in our ministry for reaching the next generation. Our creativity was a by-product of growing up in the digital culture. **(Experience "Marvelous Martha" Chapter 11 on the DVD.)**

L: As a child I was plugged into my church and the world around me. At home and in Sunday school I was learning *about* Jesus, but I yearned for an *experience* of faith in Jesus. I recall during my time as a youth director one distraught teen who shared with me that, unlike her friends, she had never "felt" the Holy Spirit. Her search for an experience that connected reminded me that I, too, wanted a sense of knowing God in ways that went far deeper than the information offered in a Sunday morning quarterly. I remember as a teenager listening to secular music and wanting to find lyrics that talked about Jesus. One song in particular is by Phil Collins, "In the Air Tonight." It's debatable whether that song is really about much of anything, other than air, as I reflect now. But when I was twelve, I heard one particular line—*I can feel it coming/In the air tonight/Oh Lord*—and was convinced that because Phil Collins sang "Oh Lord," he was a Christian and I was listening to a "Christian" song. I had a natural yearning to identify with a personality who felt something in the air. Perhaps this need is also present in the story of the Israelites in Nehemiah 8,who wanted to hear the Word of God in their own language. My adolescent question was the same question that evangelists have been posing for centuries: What experience makes religious faith intimate to the people of God?

J: At the age of eight or nine my parents bought our first home computer. It was an Atari SE. It was then that I first began to use "make-believe" characters and produce digital stories. With that first computer and my electronic drawing pad in hand, I created simple characters and animations that I would play over and over. I was completely unaware then of how valuable those hours would become in front of the computer. It was the beginning of my digital cultural training.

TV and movies are a universal part of my generation's childhood, as they were for my parents, but for me they had an exceptional impact. I wasn't very tuned into my church, and most of the time I'd sit in the back and doodle rather than listen. I could not understand why my church and more specifically the stories of the Bible could not be as compelling as the movies that I loved. Although Jesus was apparent in my life, I went to church because my parents made me attend. Most of the time I was bored, except during church camp, where for a week every story was presented in a way that made sense. After it was over I'd return to the boring "grown-up" church.

I also looked for God's presence in the stories that captivated me. Like Len, I found myself justifying how certain characters, movies, and songs were "Christian." *Star Wars* has always been one of my favorite movies. As a kid I went to see it for the first time with my family. I was thoroughly engaged and thrilled by the story. At the first part of the movie, where Luke Skywalker and Princess Leia swing across a ravine within the Death Star to escape capture by an army of storm troopers, I remember being terrified that they might not make it. I turned to my parents for reassurance, saying, "God will protect them, right, Mom?" My parents giggled and gave me the assurance I needed. Although that may be a cute reminder about the naive mind of a child, in retrospect, it shows me that, like most children from whom creativity and wonder are not yet extracted, I have a hard time separating the presence of God in my life from the stories that capture my imagination.

Can the wondrous presence of God be communicated to the digital culture in the language and imagery of story?

L: Any culture may be understood from its communication forms. Hundreds of volumes of biblical criticism are devoted to the study of narrative and mythology in ancient parallel stories. Digital culture is no different. The media of digital culture, or "digital media," is a self-descriptive codifier for the collection of a wide variety of communication forms, such as telephones, televisions, and the Internet. As discussed in Chapter 1, these forms are converging. In fact, "digital media" is a technically and culturally more accurate term for what was known as "electronic media." Technically, it is a medium that uses bytes, not atoms, as its transmitting device. Culturally, through the Internet and the rise of desktop video for the layperson, digital media is the chosen medium for a new generation that prefers interactivity to passivity.

More important, however, digital media is closely associated with an entirely new cultural paradigm that has been captured so ubiquitously in the experiential marketing of the past few years. This cultural paradigm has been closely analyzed throughout the past decade in the studies and dialogue of postmodernism. While a single chapter is limited in its ability to further the digital discussion, it is important to understand something about the building blocks of digital culture. We are primarily referring to our cultural landscape as "digital," rather than postmodern, because historical eras are not remembered best by being "post" or "pre" any other era. Their monikers reflect their technologies and their creatures, whether it is the Stone Age or the Jurassic Age. In our present state, these postmodern and digital definitions are becoming one.[3]

J: In the story *Jurassic Park*, scientists conduct the groundbreaking process of collecting prehistoric DNA samples to bring dinosaurs into our present world, back from extinction. The idea looked great in theory, and promised to be the Disneyland of the future. There was one problem: the dinosaurs weren't equipped with the instincts to exist in the world in which they found themselves. With the dinosaurs so out of their element and the scientists so unprepared for dinosaur interaction, the results were disastrous.

Whether you have dino DNA or digital DNA running through your veins, ministering to the digital culture is possible. Regardless of your makeup, to avoid such disaster, it is crucial to understand a series of important aspects of digital culture, or chromosomes, if you will. For those with digital DNA the jump is easier, but it does require some particular observation of the culture in which we live. Leaders with digital DNA will tap into experiences that are formed by growing up in digital culture. This book, and particularly this chapter are written to aid leaders with dino DNA to step into their digital transformation.

L: The following list offers a few key characteristics of digital DNA. Of course, it would be impossible to fully examine even one of these characteristics, so please pardon the compression that we apply.

Ambiguity

Our generation, commonly known as X, is the first social cohort not to be bound by a construct of objectivity. As mentioned in *The Wired Church*, one of the primary functions of media in a religious context in the twentieth century was the presentation of "Good News."[4] More than just an etymology of the word *Gospel*, the ministry notion of "good news" was a direct counter to one of the basic concepts of news, which is based on conflict. The reasoning was that the Gospel is the answer to the bad news of the world: news full of hope and goodness instead of evil and despair. This understanding of the Gospel correlated with the modern age, which believed that the notion of reason, science, and objectivity could be applied to the defense of the Gospel. As seminary taught me and so many other people, reason supports faith.

But quantum physics, relativity, and the postmodern era have permanently fractured reason and the Scientific Method as primary barometers for thought. During conference events with Michael Slaughter about the role of media and the future of the Church, we referred to the Media Reformation.[5] Mike defines postmodern as a culture that has become post-scientific. We often claim that to be effective in the communication of the Gospel ministers must understand the ambiguous nature of postmodernism and cease relying upon scientific method to overcome it.

While science will always have an important role in the development of a society's technology, it is clear that objectivity no longer defines us, as Walter Cronkite once bemoaned about contemporary news production (see Chapter 3, "Story and expository"). Yet the church continues to rely on this construct as a root for a Christian apologetics and evangelism, as if following a project plan spreadsheet will save the culture, a congregation, or a denomination. Being effective ministers in digital culture means recognizing these changes and developing a new construct for Christian apologetic that speaks to an ambiguous faith.[6]

J: Paul wrote, "Now I know in part: then I shall understand fully, even as I have been fully understood." It is that ambiguity that leads to a deeper faith. Our lack of knowledge leads to a deeper dependence on the Holy Spirit.

L: Looking back on God's preparatory actions in my life, I realize the unique nature of my place in history, bridging the two eras of postmodern and modern, objective and relative. I was born a year after the moon landing, of a father who served as pastor, schooled in old school liturgical practice. I read many books and I also watched MTV for thousands of hours. I was taught in a classic church-related liberal arts university, where computers didn't come to every student until the year after I graduated. But, while there I was part of a group of guys who both met for weekly Bible study and held all-night Nintendo parties.

During my graduate communications studies, I learned the prevailing communication theory that programming on television is simply the filler for the true commodity, the commercial. I also witnessed the arrival of the big–time corporate news/entertainment conglomeration. If there was ever any notion of objectivity in the presentation of news media, it was lost with the arrival of the vertically integrated media machine that controlled the creation, acquisition, and distribution of news events. I realized that when a conglomerate like AOL Time Warner creates a brand like Jennifer Lopez, who simultaneously has a hit movie, CD, single, and book tie-in, reviews that artist in *Time* magazine with "balance" that says nothing to hurt sales, advertises her on the WB network and then distributes both the products and the reviews to the consumer through AOL on-line, then any remnant of objectivity is truly lost.

So, objectivity in the culture is gone, and the modern era with its emphasis on reason and science with it. But, this acknowledgment of the prevalence of relativity is not acquiescence of my understanding of the truth of my faith. In fact, the truth of the Gospel and the role of Christ in my life and the world's have taken on fresh reality in my mind with its release from the constraints of modernism. Being out of these ideological boundaries gives me a fresher peek at the historical variances of belief and action that have constituted being a disciple of Christ. Ambiguity, or the acknowledgment that I don't have all the answers— in fact, I have very few answers—opens up a freedom to explore my identity as a disciple of Christ, not as a dog- matic drone for whom nothing is internalized.[7]

So, I operate out of a different construct that sees the role and purpose of digital media as separate from the role and purpose of information processing. The appropriation of digital media as a venue for my values does not deny these values but rather supports them, in being true to the Gospel as experienced aesthetically and true in the sense that through these media I continually search for means to express deep truths that I know but find difficult to articu- late by using the limited verbiage of the spoken language.

Part of this project comes out of the struggle in my life with defining a Christ-centered spirituality that can find authenticity outside the modern objective construct. One example that helps me is the art of film. Film, as a story form, has never tried to present itself under an "umbrella" of objectivity. Neither does it fit itself under the twin func- tions of news and entertainment. It may present news and it definitely must do so in an entertaining fashion, but ulti- mately its highest goal is to create a moving narrative expe- rience.

One favorite film is *The Insider*. This powerful movie is a retelling of a tobacco industry whistleblower's attempt to put the deceptions of his profession to public scrutiny, and the powers from within the news organization that he went to (CBS) that crushed the story because of the demands of power and money. This is a film about the very issue of "objectivity," and truth in news. The film itself, however, was criticized by several publications, including *Brill's Content*, for its "dramatic" license, as it freely admitted in the closing credits. How can a film about truth not get the details straight and still be credible? The filmmaker, Michael Mann, says simply that he altered some actual details of the story in order to present the ultimate truth of the story. Film critic Roger Ebert addressed this apparent inconsistency in his review of the film:

> Do these objections invalidate the message of the film? Not at all. And they have no effect on its power to absorb, entertain, and anger. They go with the territory in a docudrama like this, in which characters and narrative are manipulated to make the story stronger. The *Brill's Content* piece, useful as it is, makes a fundamental mistake: It thinks that Lowell Bergman is the hero of "The Insider" because he fed his version of events to Mann and his co-writer, Eric Roth. In fact, Bergman is the hero because he is played by Al Pacino, the star of the film, and thus must be the hero. A movie like this demands only one protagonist. If Pacino had played Mike Wallace instead, then Wallace would have been the hero . . .
>
> There is, I admit, a contradiction in a film about journalism that itself manipulates the facts. My notion has always been that movies are not the first place you look for facts, anyway. You attend a movie for psychological truth, for emotion, for the heart of a story and not its footnotes. In its broad strokes, "The Insider" is perfectly accurate: Big tobacco lied, one man had damning information, skilled journalism developed the story, intrigue helped blast it free.[8]

Ebert says that the experience contains a sum truth outside the truth of the parts. This is not just a truth that reaches the head, but also a truth that touches the heart. A truth that is comfortable, even that thrives, with spiritual ambiguity.

Metaphor

J: "What was last week's message about again? The pastor

preached on . . . um . . . it was . . . hmmm . . . . I can't seem to remember." Unfortunately, this stutter can be reality for many who reflect on the previous Sunday's sermon. It's not necessarily that the message was bad or that it was particularly boring. It's that we have a hard time keeping all of those ideas in our brains for a long time. Many times we can remember a particular verbal illustration, and maybe the sermon title, but more often than we'd like, the main ideas escape us when we try to recall them later.

How do pastors and worship leaders combat this retention problem? Here's the solution that the teams I've been part of have put into practice: metaphor. Applying a metaphor to your message simply takes the potentially abstract story or idea(s) you are working with and updates it to a present-day tangible equivalent. Substituting familiar objects, stories, and situations can make archaic and hard-to-grasp texts easy to understand and retain in our long-term memory, rather than short-term. Metaphor is the glue that makes it stick!

When we would develop a successful metaphor at Ginghamsburg Church, people in our congregation could easily recite the crux of a message months later. I heard folks talk about messages from years ago, and it was always tied to the metaphor. Using metaphor to communicate biblical stories allowed us to take what may have been hard or even impossible to understand in today's culture and update it in a way that made sense to everyday people.

During a worship service, our youth pastor was preaching on his experience as an African-American attending a largely Caucasian Christian college. He shared a story about a painting that covered one of the halls in the college. It depicted heaven and was filled with all Caucasian men. His reaction to this picture was, "Do I fit into a heaven that looks like that?" He went on to say, "I don't think that's what heaven will look like at all. All who believe will dwell there together, regardless of race, gender, age, and so on. So if segregation has no place on heaven, and we will all be living in harmony there, then why don't we just live a preview of heaven on earth?"

The team came up with the idea of creating one of those cheesy animations that run just before the movie starts at the theatre, and using that re-creation to open worship. You probably know the style well: dancing refreshments, crying babies, and ringing cell phones would work well to set the mood. So we went to the movie theater and got special permission to just watch the preview animation. I then set out to re-create that look in the animation. Len wrote some copy in the same punchy style and our audio engi-

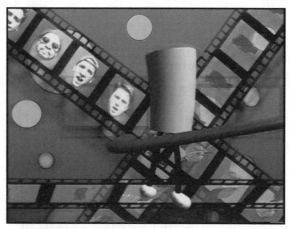

neer found the perfect announcer voice to make the audio match. We made it as close to the metaphor as we possibly could.

A woman in our congregation came to me several weeks after the celebration and said, "Jason I've got to tell you, every time I go to the movies, I think of that animation and the pastor's message. It truly reminds me to live out that preview of heaven he talked about." I knew metaphors made the message more understandable, but I never realized until then how it helped worshipers recall, with depth, the message long after it was over. We have repeatedly found that the stronger the metaphor, the stronger the sticking power.

L: Many pastors, however, have an established position toward metaphor that has been formed by a deep modern-era distrust of experience. This is because modern-era ministry split metaphors into two categories: (1) Hermeneutical metaphors, which are frequently used as illustrations in preaching, are a means of understanding doctrine. An example is the classic "bridge" metaphor of Christ's role in reconciling a fallen world to a holy God. These sorts of metaphors are largely immune to controversy. On the other hand, (2) biblical metaphors, such as a "day" in Creation, become the object of intense doctrinal debate in the modern mind.

Such metaphorical distinctions are detrimental to spiritual sensibilities in a digital culture because they devalue narrative in favor of doctrinal discussion and debate. Does it really matter how long the six time periods of Creation were? Is it not the point of the Creation story to worship the God who formed the heavens and the earth? Instead of creating division, metaphors may become opportunities for reconciliation in digital culture, as they focus on the story of God's love in Christ and not on trivial matters or intellectual gymnastics.

Somebody said to me once at a conference, "Why don't you focus less on metaphors and more on the Word of God?" The question gave me a wonderful opportunity to talk about how often the Word of God is itself metaphor. The burning bush is God in a metaphor. The dove is the Holy Spirit in a metaphor. The mustard seed is a metaphor for faith. In fact, the Word is more often communicated in metaphors than any other way that I can recall! We innately grasp understanding when a concept or object is compared (and simultaneously contrasted) to some other idea or thing in our experience. This process is the basis for abstract thinking.

When we "design" contemporary metaphors based on biblical truth, we don't expect that the metaphor will extend to every parallel facet of the biblical narrative. If such a metaphor does so, then that is an allegory, and perhaps an excess luxury. The purpose of a metaphor in worship is to provide a multifaceted point of entry by representing the basics of the biblical story in a language that the culture can understand. Perhaps, if the metaphor is at the root of the narrative, it may capture the essence of the story, but at the very least, it will create doorways through which people may pass to compare and contract the truth of the story to their experience.

Hermeneutical metaphors, however, eventually collapse when subjected to extensive analogous examination. One of our digital video experiences uses the metaphor of termites to communicate the horror of the legion of demons in the Gerasene man from the book of Mark. The metaphor of the termites isn't meant to define evil, but is simply a very present means to get a handle on the experience of evil—the way that evil eats away at our minds. **(Experience "Get Out," Chapter 10 on the DVD.)**

Story

Electronics manufacturers have been hawking "new and improved" technical miracles for a long time. One of their best achievements has yet to catch on with the American public: HDTV, or high-definition television. It has taken an act of Congress to make the public accept HDTV, because consumers don't really want better picture quality. They want better content. Technology is not the answer; in fact the ubiquity of the word *technology* itself is only evidence of the rate of modal change in our society and not a correct way to refer to what are merely the artifacts of our present culture. The paradigm shift is not about technology. It's about story.

J: One excellent episode of *Biography* on the A&E cable network told the story of the popular PBS television show *Sesame Street.* I grew up on *Sesame Street,* as did most children from my generation. The show has an incredible impact on the culture, and it changes the way that children learn.

At one point in the biography, one of the masterminds behind the success of *Sesame Street* commented that the inspiration to educate children through television was very innovative, and many felt it would fail miserably. The original goal of the show was to help children learn to count to ten and learn their ABC's. When the original pilot aired they realized a distinct flaw in its format: the educational portions were separated from the entertainment portions. This meant kids would tune out when the teachers came on, and tune back in when the Muppets returned. The test was a disaster.

The creators revamped the show. The adults on the program, who previously appeared in the educational portions of the show, now interacted with the Muppet characters. Their role was, in a sense, to be the "straight man" to the zany comedy of the Muppets. They retested the show in one hundred homes. The reviews were outstanding! The kids were glued to their TV sets. They loved it. Clearly, *Sesame Street* spoke in a language that children understand.

Soon after the show debuted on PBS, educators throughout the country had to change their curriculum. Children were walking into kindergarten ready and able to recite their ABC's, 123's and even spell simple words. The teachers, parents, and unknowingly the children, were just beginning to learn the power of what electronic culture had to offer. The goal in 2001 for *Sesame Street* is to teach children about abstract concepts like empathy. That's a lot tougher than 1+1=2, but they've harnessed the most effective medium available to reach the people of the digital age.

Educational children's shows like *Blue's Clues*, *Teletubbies*, and *Barney* have popped up everywhere. Educators now innately do what *Sesame Street* pioneered thirty years ago. Perhaps it is time for church leaders to go back to school, to learn that God's story, rather than method or systems of dogma, is the root medium for how we now understand and experience God's love.[9]

L: This understanding of digital culture is very different from the well-worn method of telling a randomly selected joke early in the sermon to get people "warmed up" to the abstract theology, or even the barnyard humor, laundry lists, and sports tales that might be strung together for a speech that works equally well before the congregation or the Kiwanis Club. Digital culture requires that we marry story to learning. Some pastors offer a rebuttal that the world doesn't need more stories; it needs "good, hard Gospel teaching." Some church leaders are convinced that developing the cultural forms of film and art somehow changes the Gospels or contaminates Christ with entertainment. This mindset divorces story from belief. But story doesn't dilute belief. It forms belief. For example, scholars have pointed out that there are parallels between the stories of the Bible and the stories or myths (which are a type of story) of ancient pagan religion. The stories of Christ have parallels with the Greek myth of Osiris. The reaction within modern-era Christianity to these sorts of proclamations was to either: (1) cease to believe in the veracity of the Bible, or (2) prove that stories are facts. Subsequently, twentieth-century Christianity split into two worlds, with redaction-critical liberals asserting that conservatives practice a fundamentalist "folk religion" and evangelical conservatives asserting that liberals have edited out the authority of the Scripture, stripped Jesus of a bodily resurrection, and succumbed to apostate lifestyles. Amid this polarized battlefield, C. S. Lewis pointed out that rather than ignore all those ancient cultural parallels that Christianity has with pagan myths, we should celebrate the convergence. It does not make Jesus any less real that there are mythological parallels to his story of death and resurrection. God used the mythological form and made it real in Christ Jesus, because God knew that humanity innately understands story more deeply than a list of propositions.[10]

Madeleine L'Engle, a celebrated Christian children's author, has this to say about story and imagination:

> Our teachers and parents tell us that what comes from our imaginations isn't true; it's just "imaginary." I think that what's imaginary is truer than what's "real." Adults prefer facts. Because facts are limited. Like truth, imagination is unlimited, so many people are afraid of it. Go outside at night in the country, where the sky is very clear. Then look up. Each one of those tiny points in the sky is a flaming sun. We're a tiny part of an enormous universe, which may be one of many universes. No one really knows for sure what's out there. So we use our imagination. Imagination allows us to ask the big questions—questions that scare us, and for which we don't have easy answers.[11]

There are conventions for telling a story, though they change to fit the genre. Most stories contain a hero, or a protagonist, who must go through a difficult journey in order to metamorphose into something new and better. In the journey are personal and social needs, or tensions, that must be confronted. For example, in the film *Erin Brokovich* the title character confronted her own sense of low self-esteem and worthlessness at the same time she confronted a corporate entity that was harming her neighbors.

Good stories have emotional, psychological, societal, and spiritual dimensions. A good story has completeness, or a definite beginning, middle, and end, which allow us to see our own place in the journey. A good story has wonder, or a sense of mystery and awe that enables us to detach ourselves from our daily lives, see connections and identify archetypes that apply not simply to the hero but to us, and others we know as well. A good story engages our senses. Finally, a good story is reflective. It has moments of silence that don't preach but allow us to ponder and absorb. (A story that captures some of these components well is **"Glimpse the Divine," Chapter 04 on the DVD.)**

Fans of doctrine may be afraid of stories because they are so inexact. But stories of and about faith don't damage faith.

As C. S. Lewis said, it would be a stumbling block to a world that innately understands the story form, if story elements were not present in religious faith. This is how people understand their commitments. Christian worship that has removed or lost awareness of story is just as dead and unappealing as a trite metaphor.

In order to make the Word into story, it is necessary first to rid the iconoclastic spirit. The commandment against graven images is not a warning against the aesthetic or the artistic, it is rather a warning against mistaken faith in a religious system where the presence, if not blessing, of God comes and goes according to the degree of faithfulness to the Law. The Incarnation redeems the story form. God now resides with us on earth in the form of the Holy Spirit, so the expressions we make are a reflection of a God that resides with us.

Story should not be confined to either a secular expression, usually a societal commentary that is devoid of spiritual meaning (think: "secular" movies), or a thinly veiled sermon with obvious, prepackaged meaning that conveys specific doctrinal agendas (think: "Christian" movies). Digital age art needs to be free in its expression of form, and allow eternal truth to come out of its creation. Artists know that one cannot control artistic creation. Our relinquishment to creativity is very unmodern but rather enabled by the Holy Spirit. Finding Christ in the freedom of expression is finding God not in dusty doctrines but in the corners of our heart and our dreams. And for the artist and the receiver, Christ is made real in our hearts and our visions of God's work in our midst.

Consider one difference between story and metaphor. You can express metaphors without stories, such as the phrase "Life is a box of chocolates." Sermons often spin off from an analysis of a metaphor. You can also have stories, very simple ones, without obvious metaphors. But, most effective are stories with strong metaphorical presence. These root metaphors are often called motifs. A motif gives context to a story and provides a means by which we can more fully understand what a story means. In the film *Forrest Gump*, the lead character contextualizes his personal story by sitting on a park bench with his own personal box of chocolates. These chocolates represent the life story he is telling to the listeners on his bench.

"Don't Hold on to Me" is based on the story of the women at the tomb who mistake Jesus for the gardener, and is told through the eyes of a young boy releasing his pet butterfly. The story of the boy letting go of his butterfly, which symbolically represents the risen Lord, provides context for the biblical story and provides a level of meaning for it that may have otherwise been lost in the usual oral scripture reading. **("Don't Hold on to Me" can be purchased at your favorite bookstore as part of** *Fresh Out of the Box: Digital Worship Experiences for Palm Sunday to Pentecost Sunday.***)**

Creativity

J: It saddens me when I hear a person say that he or she isn't creative. I think everyone is born with a creative personality trait. Some persons forget how to be creative. I don't know anyone who didn't "make believe" as a kid. Trees would become great castles, a broken branch might become a sword, and tea parties were thrown with imaginary friends. Why do we forget how to use our imaginations?

L: Maybe it's because the modern-era educational systems of our world crush it out of us at an early age. I fortunately was raised with a freedom to develop my God-given creativity. As a child my sister, Lori, and I would play newspeople. For a while when I was eight, and my father was pastor of a small United Methodist church in rural Kentucky, the two of us would create a weekly newspaper. We wrote articles, drew advertisements, and created a distribution system. The next year my father left parish ministry to rejoin his soldier brethren as a chaplain in the VA hospital system. We moved to Oklahoma City for his training. I remember Lori and I re-creating the famous radio mystery, "Sorry, Wrong Number." We produced an entire experience complete with sound effects on audiocassette and played it for our parents with the lights turned down and a candle burning for added ambience. We were fascinated with the story. **(Experience "Sorry, Wrong Number" on the DVD, under Extras.)** Also while in Oklahoma City, Lori and I hung out with my cross-town cousin a lot. One summer the three of us actually made a "movie," although we couldn't afford a home film or video camera. We developed scenes, directed ourselves, and acted them out to our parents by my aunt and uncles backyard pool.

Though I didn't realize it at the time, this creative spirit was slowly integrating with a curiosity of emerging technology. As a young teenager in Oklahoma and then in Texas we got a pre-Macintosh era Apple and an Atari 2600 game system. We were ahead of the curve in acquiring it, actually, but I wanted the technology so badly that I thought we were just about the last house in the state to get it. I was thrilled to interact with this visual medium that had formerly been presented to me in a more one-way form on our television sets. I began to associate our participatory activity of the old media forms of radio and newspaper with the early digital media activity of these games (that's all I really used the Apple for, anyway, besides drawing skylines with my sixteen color paint program). I began to see the power of this rudimentary, toddler-era medium in my own life and in the lives of my peers.

Churches are increasingly interested in digital culture technology, but are using it to solve the wrong problems, for example using scanners to capture pages from the pew Bible for projection. This amounts to designing a system to reinforce modern-era worship. Instead, brainstorm as a team on the nature of shared Gospel experience, and then create artistic representations to accommodate that imagination. These representations shouldn't be driven by technical feats, but rather formed around creative expression.

J: This process is biblical. It is no accident that the Bible starts with God modeling the creative process for us. Life, earth, existence in general, could have been created in an instant, but through the six days of the Creation story God demonstrates creativity for us. When the creative process pauses, God takes a rest. (Don't forget that part!) We're created in the likeness of God, which leads me to believe that we have the same creative abilities within us.

L: As my wife and I progress through our pregnancy, I am further reminded in many ways that to create is to be the most like God, whether it is making life or making worship art. This is not a new idea. But it does lead me to some understanding of why we're so insecure in our creative works. Of course, we are not God, and when we take on a godly behavior, we find that it is in these times that we need God the most. This need is a product of our essential separation from God, and therefore creativity is an act of spirituality.

We look to Jesus Christ in the creative act, because even as we create, we are dependant on God's guiding hand. Since we are not God, if we try to control the creative process, we suffer. It's possible that the close relationship between creativity and spirituality provides some clues as to why artists self-destruct without a God connection. They are not equipped to deal with the consequences of their creative act. But for believers, control is antithetical to the creative process. If we relinquish control of God's gift of creativity, we are free to have joy, whether in worship or in life.

Participation

J: One way to inhibit control is to focus on participation, which is important to digital-era culture. Digital DNAers, through the Internet, have had the opportunity to participate in ways that make ordinary stories extraordinarily engaging. These combined media have given viewers the chance to participate in their favorite programs. NBC's "Must See TV" ads encouraged viewers to choose the ending of one of the network's most popular sitcoms. The viewers had an opportunity to be part of the creative process.

One web site offers a new fully computer-generated movie called *Final Fantasy*. The approach gives users a chance to participate in the action. One section is devoted to the trailer for the movie, which the user designs. Participants are asked to create a title for the trailer, then pick a few key scenes and finally choose the music that would accompany the thirty-second spot. Awesome! When I finished creating my version, it began to play. It gave me a sense of what it must be like to work in Hollywood, with just a few seconds to present a new project.

Participatory worship gives worshipers the opportunity to experience Christ at a deeper level. Participation allows for hands-on experience. At conferences we often give the audience a chance to experience working in a creative team. We define the parameters of the exercise, split them into groups, and let them go at it. When the time is up we give each group the opportunity to share the creative work. Most of the time we are astonished by great ideas.

Describing participation only introduces a puzzle. Hands-on participation completes the rest of the picture. Once the team participates in creating a worship experience, they realize that this creativity is not a spectator performance, but creativity (new life!) should actually interact within the congregation during worship. If a pastor only talks *at* a congregation all morning long, and never gives the congregation the chance to share in what he or she is talking about, then there may be no reference when people try to incorporate the message into their daily routine.

L: Participation is key to effective communication and learning in the digital age. For example, take the use of paraverbals, such as "OK" or "uh-huh." To evoke a paraverbal while listening isn't necessarily to say "yes" or "no," but just to say, "I hear you." It's an encouragement to the speaker. Studies have shown that the effectiveness of communication skyrockets when the use of paraverbals is utilized because it keeps the stress level of the speaker down and therefore articulation high, and allows for a participatory response in the receiver.[12] The black church knows this well—an *Amen* isn't so much a state of lexical meaning ("so be it") as it is a response of encouragement to stimulate better communication.

A major step toward participatory worship is a move away from the idea of revered silence throughout the worship experience, which often translates to disconnectedness and incomprehension, and to encourage an atmosphere of participatory response, whether it is via paraverbals, laughter, applause, or spoken word. This doesn't mean you completely lose the function of silence in worship; there are appropriate times for each. But get people to use their vocal cords if you want participatory digital culture worship.

J: When I was thirteen I met my youth pastor. It was through his understanding of youth culture that I began to see who God really was. He would teach by using drama, humor, overhead projector art, and video. This is in my mind the first demonstration of what "culturally relevant" worship was all about.

(*L:* "Culturally relevant" is a term that has met with some resistance by well-minded advocates of "countercultural" Christianity. The difference, of course, is to be "in it" and not "of it." As Len Sweet describes, like a sailboat in water, the church needs to be in the water, but not so much a part of it that it takes on the lake and sinks. Rather, its "airy abstractions" should raise it up out of the water like a hovercraft, rising above culture.[13])

J: Worship like that connected with me and gave me a vision for how I might use my artistic gifts in ministry. My youth pastor put me to work creating artwork for T-shirts, allowed me to write and perform drama sketches, and also gave me and other youth the opportunity to plan events. He created a digital cultural environment for me by empowering me to participate in the act of ministry.

Team

L: Digital culture is defined by decentralized power. Nicholas Negroponte says that moderns are "strongly conditioned to attribute complex phenomenon to a controlling agency."[14] Most of us have grown up in a culture, or in the fumes of a culture that organized itself either under hierarchies or the leadership of a central, charismatic leader. In fact, the enduring cultural phenomenon of conspiracy theory is a by-product of modern-era organizational management, which centralizes power. One of the reasons the TV show *The X-Files* is so popular, and so characteristic of an emerging digital culture, is that it is a deconstruction of the myth of a controlling agency, or a controlling person. Whether the one in charge is in government or the church, the show repeatedly demonstrated that power corrupts. So don't trust the authorities in charge, but instead trust the intuition of the team.

Digital culture people, or digerati, understand that the

primary organizational model of the twentieth century is not the only viable social model. Consider a flock of geese. Although they fly in a "V" wedge, the one in the middle isn't the boss. Rather, the direction of the flock is the response of a collection of individual behaviors. Similarly, digital culture is about the emergence of coherence from a consensus of individual behavior. Consensus, which always seemed so impossible in a modern-era culture that empha- sized ego and individual power, suddenly becomes both possible and exciting in a group dynamic that values what is right and best over whose idea it was. Decentralized power means that not every decision must go through a central agent. Individuals who form flat team structures have the autonomy to make decisions among themselves. From this collection, teams evolve over time. Attempts to control the team process only serve to kill it.

J: In the mid 1980s I remember watching "Behind the Scenes" specials about the teams who created the *Star Wars* trilogy. Industrial Light and Magic, the team responsible for the films' special effects, intrigued me. Watching them talk about and then create complex effects shots was inspiring. Early on when they would do an effects shot (which usually meant blowing something up), they would gather up every- one in the building to come and watch. Everyone from the pyrotechnicians to the administrative assistants would cele- brate together when it was all over. Everyone felt ownership in the experience, which fueled each individual to return to his or her own responsibilities with pride and commitment. Joining in the experience helped them see that their part affected the whole project.

These early digital DNAers thrived on collaboration. They felt at home within a group of highly motivated, like- minded people. I doubt the ILM team would have said they were trying to demonstrate the body of Christ, but their col- laboration inspires the same attitude. Each member of a dig- ital age design team has a part to play in the body of the experience. With God being the head we are free to do our part to create worship experiences that are meaningful and effective. Each responsibility, from preaching, to music, to administration, to media is of equal importance. I was lucky enough to serve on a team at Ginghamsburg where team members felt that way. Pastor Mike Slaughter would often say to me that he felt my artistic gifts were as important as his gift of preaching. That attitude may be rare for ministers who serve primarily outside a team, but it is an attitude that must be learned and exhibited to function within a digital culture team.

As Len wrote in *The Wired Church*, "Don't do this alone. Don't even try."[15] Planning worship with the intent of reaching this culture is much too hard to do alone. A flat structure is important to allow for maximum creativity. This gives everyone an equal voice during the brainstorming process. The collective ownership of putting together worship in a team makes implementing it much fun.

L: But, it is said, "there must be a leader." Of course. People want to point to a leader, and leaders more often than not need to be seen as such. In fact, some leaders will apply team rhetoric to what is essentially a singular vision so long as the notion of a team doesn't interfere with individual power. But this misses the point. A pastor will not lose his or her authority as the leader of the church community because of the emergence of team. On the contrary, the vision and tenacity to oversee team development, and representation of the team through the preaching and leadership function of being a pastor, only serve to enhance a pastor's credibility in digital culture. Digital culture simply changes the leadership function. A good model for digital culture leadership is found in Pastor Wayne Cordeiro, who leads a large church in Oahu based on a decentralized, team structure.[16] At his church, you won't find Cordeiro referring to himself as "senior" pastor or using language that lifts himself up.

Digital culture people are entrepreneurial; they seize their opportunities irrespective of age or position. Young people don't have to wait thirty years to move up the hierarchical chart until they can finally pursue an avocation. As someone who is still paying off school loans years after finishing my graduate degree, I don't necessarily like the bondage of debt any more than most moderns heavily invested in hierarchical systems. But the reality is that in our new culture authority doesn't come from a degree, a position of authority, or a role as teacher. It comes from experience, passion, and the ability to articulate a vision. Leadership is function, not position. For people to be experts, it is not just because they are well read on the subject, but because they have been there. They are practitioners.

Unfortunately, the church is still bound by the vertical organizational models of modern culture. This creates a condescending attitude among those who have "put in the time" following modern-era organizational movement, and only ends up driving away good digital talent from the church.

Experience

J: People in digital culture aren't looking for information about God. They are looking for an experience of God. Billions of dollars are spent every year to hook consumers on various products, through interactive and experiential marketing. Nearly every auto commercial now is centered on the idea of giving drivers a multisensory experience. Pounding music, inspiring visuals, and tag lines rooted heavily in experience, run rampant as you flip through your 100-plus channels. And now, with the Internet in full swing, TV is only part of the whole plan. Marketing directors know full well that this culture wants an experience, and so promotional campaigns have been stepped up several notches to meet the demands of an emerging digital culture.

BMW's newest campaign is a prime example of what this type of culture looks like. I was sitting in my easy chair a few weeks ago when I saw what I thought was a trailer for a new movie called *Ambush*. The action was excellent and the stunts incredible; it was scored like a film. At the end of the spot I was waiting to find out when the film came out, and to my surprise, it ended with graphics saying: Only at bmw-films.com.

Well, it didn't take but a few minutes for me to fire up the computer and begin my interactive experience. What I found when I got there was even more fun. I was directed to download the free BMW interactive film player to see the rest of the film. After the download was complete, I started the player and my screen was taken over by an interface that made my screen look like a display from a sci-fi movie. The interface, filled with cool buttons and visuals, allowed me to (in a sense) control the action. Next to a "download Ambush" button was a description of the story line that recapped the TV spot. It read: "On a dark freeway, a van swerves close to The Driver and the door slides open. From inside, masked gunmen threaten to open fire unless The Driver surrenders his passenger, a seemingly harmless man they accuse of smuggling diamonds. It's a simple choice: do or die." After downloading, I played the film.

The six-minute film was fantastic. It then occurred to me once it was over that I'd not heard one word about BMW. I didn't even know what model car he was driving. Instead, the experience provided me with a feeling that I knew how a BMW might handle around tough turns. I remember thinking at one point, *Yeah, right! Like the brakes on my car are that good. Are they really that good on BMW's?* Instead of pontificating about how great their cars are, and what features you get when you buy a BMW, they impressed me with a lasting experience.

I've never thought about owning a BMW. I can't afford a BMW. I had not until that day been even remotely interested in their web site or product. But they hooked my imagination because they understand how a digerati, or digital culture person, thinks.

BMW isn't alone in its endeavors to reach us with experiential marketing. Companies like iFilm.com and atom films are fully web-based, hoping to give audiences an experience that will make them come back again and again. Their sites give users the opportunity to be entertained, educated, and participate by rating movies, writing reviews, and so on.

L: The move from analysis to experience is the most important distinction between modern and digital culture, and the one that is often the most difficult for moderns to grasp. I have found in speaking during one-day seminars that it frequently takes us several times to communicate this difference, and from several angles, before it is fully understood.

Consider the use of film clips in a worship setting. Are

they to be used as a shared experience or as an illustration for the lesson of the day? Or, should they be a teaching metaphor or a metaphor that captures the essence of a story? Modern-era pastors might be tempted to follow a film clip in worship with a question like, "What do you think of the question John asked?" or, "John represents Jesus, etc." *It is trite and clichéd to use a teaching ploy like that*, thinks the digital culture person. Digerati often see right through such a ploy because they would rather participate in forming the worship than in opening mouths for a spoon-fed lesson for the day.

On the other hand, perhaps in the midst of a talk about his or her personal experiences related to a subject, a speaker stops to show a clip that says the same thing in its unique way, and then returns to his or her own story. In this case the clip becomes an experience, a story within the story, and not an illustration for the lesson of the day. For example, the movie *Shrek* has a superb scene that captures the fear of loneliness and rejection. A speaker talking about the need for community might refer to their own experience of rejection and then seamlessly show the clip of the ogre Shrek opening up to his friend Donkey about his fear of rejection. The clip need not "preach" a point because it demonstrates very effectively that we all need community.

The mind-set of "a lesson a day" is referenced in *The Wired Church* as an "AV mentality," whether done orally, read, or presented through a film clip. Digital culture requires a presentation of experience that is mutually shared, through which the Holy Spirit may move, imparting each one with the comfort and wisdom of God.

Preachers are learning that the length of footnotes, the rhyme or alliteration of three-points, or the size of one's words doesn't impress congregations that thrive in the digital culture. With limited time to prepare sermons each week, why spend an hour finding an illustration from *Time* magazine to support the lesson for the day? It seems fruitful to spend more time living and reflecting upon one's own faith journey, and share out of this experience. It's not possible to wrap up all the answers in twenty-five minutes, like a TV sitcom. Instead, by finding narratives in digital culture that articulate the pastor's personal journey, the congregation is invited to participate in their own stories, which gives the entire community deeper insight into the ongoing movement of God and comfort of the Holy Spirit.

Five components of experience

In *Experiential Marketing*,[17] the author articulates a typology to replace the "features and benefits" approach to advertising, which has dominated marketing theory for the past twenty years. His typology is applicable not only to the design of marketing for digital culture, but also to the design of worship for digital culture. Of course, worship is meant to be a much more ultimate experience than viewing a TV ad, and its purpose is to create disciples not consumers (which are very different objectives!). The church would be remiss to ignore the opportunity to redeem the effectiveness of experiential persuasion for a higher purpose. The author, Bernd Schmitt, defines five experiential components, or what he calls "strategic experiential modules (SEMs)." These SEMs are *sense, feel, think, act,* and *relate.* As I put these SEMs in the context of worship, think about your responses and share them with your worship colleagues at the next design session.

Sense strategies engage the five human senses of sight, sound, smell, taste, and touch. The objective of sensory strategies, according to Schmitt, is to "provide aesthetic pleasure, excitement, beauty and satisfaction through sensory stimulation."[18] Sensory experiences have high impression value. They often include fast-paced and movement pieces, and are designed to motivate us and to demonstrate superior value. A classic sense example is the thrill of Mountain Dew ads. I particularly like the one where the biker chases down the cheetah that has swallowed his can of Dew.

The best *sense* experiences are integrated—that is, they appeal to more than one sense at the same time. They also have what Schmitt calls "cognitive consistency" because they follow a stylistic and thematic order, so that our brains process similarities between the various stimuli. Otherwise, a bombardment on our senses quickly disintegrates into clutter (which aptly describes some attempts at "contemporary" worship). Of course, the "Information Age" is founded on sensory overload. We have new drugs created now especially for children who become overstimulated. So part of *sense* is salience; that is, high contrast to its received surroundings. The first Christmas TV spot I ever created as a media minister was salient, with no voiceover or score for an audio track, but only sound effects. The purpose was to catch TV audience attention. In an age of overstimulation, *sense* may mean silence, especially the kind of sudden silence where you can hear the air rush in your ears.

Consider parallels between the *sense* SEM and the worship traditions of the Roman Catholic Church, which attempt to capture the mystery of God through the use of such sensory artifacts as incense, cathedrals, and the Eucharist. The recent term "multi-sensory" worship captures this mystery by focusing on high sensory experience, which is one way to interact with digital culture. This parallel between ancient and future sensory experiences may help to explain reports that large numbers of boomers and Gen X young adults returned to Roman Catholic churches in the 1990s.

When analyzing worship according to sensory stimulation, sensory experiences must be judged as a whole and not individually. Nicholas Negroponte describes an early HDTV experiment that had two focus groups watch the same movie on the same television set, one with a high-quality surround sound stereo system and the other with a low-quality mono sound system. All other factors being equal, the former group perceived they were watching a higher resolution television. Changing the sound changed the perceived visual experience. The study proved that people judge their experiences as a sensory whole and not by individual elements of sight, sound, touch, taste, or smell.[19]

Feel strategies appeal to our feelings and are designed to affect, to create specific emotional responses. My favorite examples are Hallmark ads and Mormon ads. Schmitt points out that proper use of feel in advertising targets the emotional state of someone during "consumption." While that word may cause a negative effect in you the reader, the lesson is worth learning. It is in the act of feeling things, not thinking about them, that we have our strongest emotional states. Feel strategies relate to emotions as we are experiencing them.

Recall the controversy around a Super Bowl ad a couple of years ago that showed the paralyzed Christopher Reeve standing up and walking. The ad was extremely effective, causing some people to react against its unfulfilled promises and others to find hope in its optimism. *Feel* has great ability for both hope and cynicism. It must be approached carefully in worship. Worship, as we will explore more in Chapter 3, is more than the elicitation of a specific spiritual emotion or mood. Much of contemporary worship does damage to a congregation's perception of the worship act and one's relationship to God by focusing on emotional highs.

On the other hand, emotions are a natural part of a worship experience. They will occur whether we intend them to or not. Sometimes, in fact, emotions may lead a congregation away from the intended direction. Complex psychology informs each of our affective experiences. For example, as the son of an officer who served in Vietnam, I have a complex reaction to the presence of an American flag during worship. My feelings about the mixture of Christianity and patriotism, about church and state, may be very different from the person beside me, or even from the intentions of the worship planner. This reaction has been made more complex by the recent terrorist attacks.

How does a digital age worship planner deal with *feel*? The answer comes through openness to affective response in our simple telling of the Gospel through story form.

Think strategies appeal to our intellect. They are cognitive experiences, which provide opportunities to address major issues, both personal and societal. They have components of surprise, intrigue, and provocation. My favorite *think* ad is Accenture's "Now things get interesting." One ad in their campaign said, "Chinese will become the number one web language by 2007. Now things get interesting." Another famous *think* ad is Microsoft's "Where do you want to go today?"

How does *think* fit into the digital age? Doesn't it lend itself to modern, abstract critical analysis such as we recall in the liberal Protestant tradition? According to Schmitt, *think* is not analytical reasoning, which can destroy experiences (paralysis by analysis), but a divergent thinking that is more free form and creative in nature. It is like brainstorming. It invites people to deviate into entirely new realms of thought around a particular subject. For example, as an imitation of Accenture's campaign, I might say, "There are 350,000 churches in the United States. There are 3,000 musicians studying organ in universities . . . . Transforming worship for the digital age."

Think tactics may work best in two aspects of a traditional worship structure: the call to worship and the sermon. A call to worship or sermon opener may act as an attention-getter, engaging the congregation to evaluate their lives or the world. By creating a state of openness, they are able to freely brainstorm how a relationship with Jesus and a community of believers might change their lives.

Act strategies attempt to respond to physical desire by invoking changes in our behavior and lifestyle. Schmitt points out that the classic act campaign is Nike's "Just Do It," which transformed viewers' perceptions of exercise. Act, of course, is the goal of most sermons: to invite changed lives, accept Christ, serve in some capacity, cease sin, develop a positive self-perception in Christ, and so forth. Effective action in worship invites the congregation to experience the lifestyle change of being a follower of Christ. Bonhoeffer's *The Cost of Discipleship*, which is often quoted in sermons about cheap grace, is a classic example of guiding believers to act.

Relate strategies draw from the other four modules but expand beyond individual experience, creating social systems based on relationships with other people or cultures. Relate strategies draw upon our innate search for belonging and meaning. In this case, parallels are obvious within Christianity, which is essentially a relational religion. When we are called to follow Christ, we are called to engage those around us with love. Worship can accomplish that through simple acts of "passing the peace" or greeting your neighbor, or through more complex presentations of missions or acts of mercy.

Holistic DNA

J: Known as a double helix, DNA is shaped like a twisted ladder. The rungs of this ladder carry the genetic information that forms a person. All rungs must be present for the DNA to be complete. As you move ahead into digital age worship, be sure all the DNA rungs are present.

L: The presence of each rung creates a whole entity. In the same way, these digital DNA are not meant to exist separately, as in, "Oh, we have a story this week, so we're reaching digital culture!" These are meant to exist together. Each of these characteristics, as outlined in this chapter, is a part of the double helix of digital culture. Together they form a new framework for how we might pursue an effective ministry.

For example, each of Schmitt's modules has a place in the communication structure of digital culture, and in digital age worship. Digital age worship may contain elements of any or all of these characteristics: it may focus on a story told with graphics and video, or it may be low-technology but highly participatory. It may take on many styles or mediums, but it is only authentic to our digital age if it demonstrates these DNA.

3. Leonard Sweet, *Soul Tsunami: Sink or Swim in New Millennium Culture* (Grand Rapids: Zondervan, 2000), p. 29.
4. Len Wilson, *The Wired Church: Making Media Ministry* (Nashville: Abingdon, 1999), p. 21.
5. Michael Slaughter, *Out on the Edge: A Wake Up Call for Church Leaders on the Edge of the Media Reformation* (Nashville: Abingdon Press, 1998).
6. Kevin Graham Ford, *Jesus for a New Generation* (Downers Grove: InterVarsity, 1995). A great read for more insight on reaching The Generation Formerly Known As "X."
7For more reading on Gen X spirituality, see Tom Beaudonin, *Virtual Faith: The Irreverent Spiritual Quest of Generation X.* (New York: Jossey-Bass, 1998).
8. Roger Ebert review on http://www.suntimes.com, Nov. 5, 1999.
9. By downgrading method or dogma we don't mean to minimize the importance of Christian practices, which are experienced as behavioral disciplines, such as the means of grace or acts of piety: prayer, Bible reading, caring for the suffering, and so on.
10. "Myth Matters," by Louis A. Markos. *Christianity Today,* April 23, 2001, pp. 32-39.
11. "Where Do Good Ideas Come From?" Bernd Auers, *American Way,* June 2000, p. 94.
12. Nicholas Negroponte, *Being Digital* (New York: Alfred A. Knopf, 1995), p. 142.
13. Sweet, *Soul Tsunami,* p. 21.

14. Negroponte, *Being Digital*, p. 167.

15. Wilson, *The Wired Church: Making Media Ministry*, p. 75.

16. For more information on this successful model, read Wayne Cordeiro, *Doing Church as a Team* (Gospel Light Publishing, 2000), a source of information about how New Hope Christian Fellowship of Hawaii succeeds by using a flat team structure.

17. Bernd, Schmitt, *Experiential Marketing: How to Get Customers to Sense, Feel, Think, Act and Relate to Your Company and Brands*. (New York: The Free Press, 1999.)

18. Ibid, p. 99.

19. Negroponte, *Being Digital*, pp. 125-26.

Chapter 3
The Art of Communicating the Gospel

J: The screen, as described in Chapter 1, has been limited to an AV approach for displaying song lyrics, points, and scriptures, announcements, and various forms of information. This limitation turns the potentially powerful screen into a tiresome and uninspiring medium. We have a choice as media producers to be information providers or artistic inspirers.

There is a very strong emphasis on racial reconciliation at the church where I served, and Martin Luther King Jr. weekend reflects that passion. On this particular weekend in January, a guest speaker shared a message with us that he called "Sprinkle the Blood." He drew parallels between the death of Abel in Genesis 4:10 ("The voice of your brother's blood is crying to me from the ground"), the death of Martin Luther King Jr., and ultimately the blood of Christ that was shed at the cross. Our typical response as human beings when reacting to senseless deaths might be to ask, "Why, God?" But through Christ's blood, we are convinced to serve a God who is greater than the enemy.[20]

It was my challenge to present this idea as an image. The graphic, in subtle ways, points to MLK, and in more obvious ways to the death of Christ. I chose to use a stark contrast of black and white and selective red coloring for the blood on the cross and theme words. The process of building the graphic was simple, but the power of the viewing experience was more than I could have expected.

An African-American woman who knew that I created graphics for worship approached me following the service. She told me that she could not look at it without her eyes filling with tears. She said, "Your image made it too real."

A less artistic approach might result in a bland graphic. This second image communicates the same information and has an identical color mix to the first, but fails to evoke the same emotive response that the former image does.

L: Lasting knowledge of any era is a reflection of that era's art. From stories told around the campfires of oral tradition to the finest works in the Louvré, the best of artistic expression for every age is both a commentary on the times in which it was made and a meditation on the universal human condition.

More important, however, in very specific ways art is one of the primary means through which we can encounter God. How, you may ask? First, art reminds us of *what is real.* When we have opportunities to strip away falsehoods from our lives, we are able to see *reflections of God* in the world. The very nature of art is a way in which we may see both the presence of God and a glimpse of the depth of God's love for us. This, of course, may only occur when the art has meaning. Art, someone told us at a conference, is only art when it creates a response in its receiver. When it is *rooted in the culture* in which it is made. *Discipleship begins* in this moment of response and understanding, and it happens in the form of questions; *questions we ask* of ourselves and our world around us. These questions form faith in us, which both *heals us* and begins to erase, or *transcend, the boundaries* that divide us from other people. And when we begin to love others as we love ourselves, we are more prepared to *encounter the abiding love of God*. So let's look at each of these components separately. Art . . .

. . . is a reminder of what's real

Art and our created world are closely linked. My wife and I bought our first house and got pregnant with our first child in the span of nine months. This intense learning curve made me realize that basic life skills are seriously undervalued in our compartmentalized, digital society. We live in a highly specialized, highly interdependent world. (This is why films like *Cast Away* and *Office Space* and TV shows like *Survivor* are so successful: they play off the same fantasy as *Robinson Crusoe*, which for three hundred years has been providing people with a vision of what it would be like to find purpose and meaning in the basics of hunting and foraging in an ancient tribal society.)

Stop for a moment and think about your life this day. Think about what you ate. Look at the roof over you. Did someone else catch, grow, or prepare your lunch? Do you work and live in a shelter built and possibly even maintained by another? Likely, on both counts. Sometimes we even have others raise our children. Meanwhile, we go about the business of our highly specialized jobs.

The role of religion, of finding meaning, value, and purpose to our lives in such a world as this is drastically different from in the world of the Bible. In the preindustrialized world, specifically the ancient world, religion was much more basic. Ancient gods and mythologies provided answers to the basic questions of whether the community was going to have a harvest come fall. Nomadic tribes worshiped fertility gods out of the fear of the unknown future. In this environment, the God of the Hebrew people, Yahweh, was different from other gods. Yahweh was a God who wanted relationship with people. This God would take care of people's needs, without bribery or begging, but Yahweh's plans were much greater than just the basics of life. These plans included not just subsistence but also meaning and purpose.

Unlike in ancient times, we live in a world in which we don't really have to worry about basics like food and shelter, or even infant mortality. Our dependency on Yahweh is much more subtle. Our narrow life focus means that we often miss out on the important things in life, to say nothing about ignorance about how the basics of life actually work. Art reminds us of what is real in our highly specialized world. It reveals God to us.

. . . is a reflection of God

After each creative moment, or day, Genesis says that God stops and ponders the created world. Each moment, God says, is good. Creation reflects God, and it has purpose and beauty. As part of the Creation, and as ones created in the image of God, we are made to be creators, or artists, as well. The very fact that we exist in God's Creation and create in our own right gives us the chance to do the one thing that most clearly glorifies and reveals the wonder of God. The better our creations, the more fully we reveal God to the world.

J: Being created in the likeness of God means that each of us has an innate ability to create art in one form or another. Some of us have just forgotten how. As children, I'd venture to say that all of us were wildly creative. That same creativity, through the power of the Holy Spirit in our lives, can be used to create art that reflects the Creator.

I find that as I'm creating artwork for worship, I often come to a place where I am unclear about how to proceed. Although I often begin by praying for the Spirit's guidance, I still face hurdles along the way. I've heard pastors pray, "Let my words be your words." As an artist I feel that same responsibility when I pray, "Let my strokes be your strokes as I render this piece." God is always faithful. Most of the time I can look back on the art I've created and see where God has given me direction when I was lost. The "footprints in the sand" cliché is true for me as an artist. I feel closest to God when I am in the middle of the creative process. What comes out on the other side is always more than I am capable of as an artist on my own. I can see God in the works I create because I know when it wasn't me doing the painting on the digital canvas.

Further, as a participant in worship, I see God reflected when I am touched at an emotive level through such media as imagery on the screen, characters in a drama, or in music being shared. Sometimes I walk into a sanctuary and look at the screen and I am filled with that "butterfly" feeling. It's as if the Spirit is joyfully stirred when such a vivid depiction is made to worshipers.

Since we are created in the likeness of God, our creations point back to the Creator, whether the artist realizes it or not. Even the most secular artists have been created with God's creative qualities; many times their work is a powerful reflection of the source of that gift. For example, although most Hollywood features are not "Christian" in nature, many have helped me see God's truth in ways more "real" than that displayed by modern-era sermons on the same subjects.

Dead Man Walking for instance, is one of the most powerful expressions of Christlike forgiveness I've ever seen. It caused me to ask some deep questions about how far I am willing to go when others have done me wrong.

Another prime example is the movie *Contact*, based on the novel written by atheist Carl Sagan. This movie explores science and faith in things unseen. Jodie Foster plays Ellie Arroway, an astronomer whose life has been dedicated to proving the existence of intelligent life elsewhere in the universe. Her character discovers a signal coming from space that contains plans for a craft that will make it possible to visit the signal's origin twenty-five light-years away. The spacecraft only has room for one, and Ellie becomes a candidate for the job of interstellar representative. Along the way she meets an unconventional priest (Mathew McConaughey) who is also an adviser to the government on the mission. He and Ellie form a relationship and discover that their views on God are very different. Ellie does not believe in God or the supernatural. This becomes a problem when the selection begins for who will go on the mission. McConaughey's character and much of the world believe that the representative should believe in God, and so he is forced to advise against sending her.

When a zealous protestor sabotages the mission and destroys the craft, killing the person chosen to represent the earth, Arroway is chosen to make the journey. She enters the craft, and in an instant is transported to an incredible place called Vega. But when she returns, she finds that her mission has been labeled a failure. What seemed like hours to her was only a few seconds to the rest of the world. When she is asked to account for what happened, she cannot. Science fails her, and she is forced to turn to faith to describe her experience.

Sagan's story, whether intended or not, makes a case for faith in God, and provides us with an experience where our own faith can be strengthened through the questions asked in the film. These faith issues dealt with in *Contact* were developed in a "secular" film but ultimately point many of us to God.

In spite of such opportunities for self-reflection, some feel that secular films have no place in worship. When truth is present in the films we see, we must remember that all truth is God's truth. Jerry Solomon and Jerry Williams write, "The dichotomy between sacred and secular is alien to biblical faith.[21] Paul's statement, 'Unto the pure, all things are pure' (Titus 1:15) includes the arts. While we may recognize that human creativity, like all other gifts bestowed upon us by God, may be misused, there is nothing inherently more sinful about the arts than other areas of human activity." God's truth is present in art, at times despite the artist.

It's amazing to me how God is revealed through art, even when unexpected. I've been part of some disastrous worship services that I didn't think could be used to glorify God but in the end God acted. At another memorable weekend a worship service focused on unity in Christ. God's intent for humanity has been to be a single community, in life and faith, but the world's brokenness has fractured this ideal. I set out to create two animations that would show that brokenness and then ultimately show how through Christ's sacrifice we may be reconciled to each other and to God.

Several diverse hands reach out to break bread together. The picture is treated like a painting. As the worship host shares the call to worship the "painting" begins to move, separating into a jumbled mess of puzzle pieces. Later in the service, during Communion, the pieces are fused back together, restoring the picture that the Artist created.[22]

Though the animation appeared to hit the mark, ironically, the production process was very painful. First, when we got the group of hands together to take the picture for the graphic, the camera wouldn't work. Then there was the bread, the central focus of the piece. Upon initial investigation none could be found, in a large church with regular Communion! Someone went to the freezer and found an old, stale loaf and brought it to us. Unfortunately, it was partially covered in mold, but we could get the shot. Then, while creating the background I dropped a slide projector and broke its bulb. At this point I wondered if I should just give up. I turned to the animation, setting up the 3-D files and starting the final render process (this is where the computer combines all of the elements into a final video sequence). The piece was so complex that it crashed my computer repeatedly over the two days it took to finish. When I saw the final results, all I saw were mistakes. There were strange anomalies caused by the computer problems I had along the way, which caused frames to skip and flicker. I didn't want to use it and was embarrassed to show the team the first time. Even as we ran it the first time in worship I was afraid it would distract more than it would help communicate the message. Then, as the host shared the call to worship in sync with the video, I saw God's presence shining through despite my worries. The things I don't like about that piece have always been overshadowed by the reflection of God that is present in the art.

. . . is rooted in culture

L: Art is not the pretty picture that we hang on our walls. It is not eye candy. The power of art is found in its ability to make people see the same thing in new ways. Its nature, therefore, is to be on the front edge of understanding. When we get familiar with an object, it loses its power, or meaning, in our lives. Art opens our eyes again. However, art can't do that if it is so esoteric that it has no meaning for us. To truly be art, any creation must be rooted in its indigenous culture. This is so important, and so misunderstood by the church, that we've devoted the entire next chapter to it.

... is more than evangelism; it's the discovery of discipleship

Currently, art and religion most often meet in the form of evangelism. To many circles in the church, the validity of art is found in the clarity of its Gospel presentation. If it walks the viewer through the four spiritual laws, then it is good art. Agendas pervade "Christian" art. What makes something "Christian"? Is it the clarity of Gospel presentation? Or is it *mise-en-scène*, the film term for the collection of people and artifacts that make up the meaning of the composed frame in any given scene or scenes? Is an image Christian because it is full of Christians? To say something is "Christian" at all connotes a worldview that sees the culture of Christianity as separate, as discussed later. Though the roots of the separatist tradition run much deeper, much of the current attitude comes from modernism, when much of Christianity assumed a defensive stance in response to the questioning nature of humanism.

Art doesn't need to be explicitly "Christian." Good art simply points people to Jesus Christ the Savior and Jesus Christ the embodiment of fully human, redeemed Person because of its ability to speak to the human condition. That is why the scene of Indiana Jones stepping out into the chasm[22] is such a popular movie in worship services about faith, because we all have moments, pre-Christians included, where life necessitates a blind step. Art is deeper than its singular ability to lead people into a new relationship with Christ. We have to realize that as we tell the truth about how God has changed and is changing the world through the redemptive act of Jesus Christ, the agenda will take care of itself.

Art is powerful when it evokes the spiritual act of becoming more transformed into the likeness of Christ. It is a reminder of what's really important about life, and how it all fits together, what is meaningful, and what matters. Art makes us laugh and cry. It stirs the character in us that forms who we are. This includes displays of love, compassion, and honor. Art reminds us of the hunger in both our body and our soul: voids that only Jesus Christ can fill. Art awakens in us the things we suppress and points us to our Savior. Art gives us meaning. I don't mean doctrinal meaning, or "head truth." I mean the kind of discovery that is an act of discipleship. It is not understanding the details of a doctrinal position based on the illustration of a current event that grows the Spirit of Christ within us, it's our discovery of the nature of loving others, of following Jesus, of faith and risk, and commitment to love.

I anticipate that each of us has at least one particular moment we can recall when art has helped the formation of Christ within us. One of my life themes is courage. The film *Braveheart* helped me to define that the presence of Christ in me stirs me to act on the courage of sacrifice, and that being Christlike is not passive, but boldly compassionate and courageous.

Question:

What is your moment?
Log on to www.abingdonpress.com/ebooks and tell your own story of art as discipleship, on the message board.

J: Kasey is a youth pastor at a midsize church near St. Louis. At the top of her list of needs is discipleship. She observes that heavily programmed events are not the priority they once were in youth ministry. Discipleship begins when the message is understood. What we do with artistic presentation of the Bible meets youth where they are. We tell the stories of the Gospel in a language that they already understand, which is step one in beginning a walk with Christ.

One children's ministry teacher wasn't sure she liked this new "gimmick" of media in worship. She was concerned that it was just entertainment. When she decided to test her theory, an amazing thing happened. The teacher asked her students what worship was about the previous week, and the kids gave a description that sounded as if it was about their favorite cartoon. They remembered every nuance. The teacher was impressed, but still skeptical. She repeated the drill the following week, and the results were the same. It wasn't long before this skeptic became an advocate for these new Gospel communication forms. The children began to know the stories of the Bible and the teacher started to incorporate digital age teaching forms. Discipleship was triggered by art.

. . . raises questions

L: Art also raises deep questions. From individual to universal, we find what is true in all of us through what is true for one. By connecting with what we know, we can move beyond to what we do not yet know. In this act, we begin to ask questions of ourselves and the world around us. It is in this state of questioning that we find growth. This growth both heals our broken spirits and makes us aware of others around us and in the world who need similar healing.

J: Art is more easily open for interpretation, in the minds of many churched leaders, than are the creedal words or memorized Scriptures that we recite. This means that worshipers can draw additional meanings from images used to communicate the Gospel. Many times a viewer will point out their favorite part of an image, and I am stunned at their interpretation. Things that I didn't even consciously render have the most profound impact.

When we survey churches we find that their opinions and interpretations are widely diverse. One user will name a favorite graphic and the next will say the same graphic is the one they dislike the most.

Additionally, art can bring layers of meaning to a worship experience. Since art is an interpretive medium, individual worshipers may experience the Gospel in different ways. What speaks to me may not speak to the person sitting next to me, and the person sitting behind me in worship may see something completely different from both of us. The interpretive nature of art allows for worshipers to draw contextualized application from the visual presentation of the Gospel. This approach does not force-feed one viewpoint but allows for unique individual experiences. The interpretation of art can raise questions and evoke emotions that can be addressed by the pastor's message (which is open for interpretation, too, of course).

. . . has the power to heal

Art has the power to heal both in a physical and an emotional sense. I recall a TV program about music therapy on CBS's, *48 Hours*. They featured a clinic, the Center for Music

Therapy in Austin, Texas, which uses music to teach people with debilitating injuries to communicate and walk again. One man had been in a car accident and sustained injuries so severe that he was initially unable to speak and walk. The center's program of therapy taught this man to sing and to walk to the beat of music with incredible results. He could not clearly speak even a sentence, but he could sing along as the therapist played songs on the guitar. And although he struggled to walk, when given headphones and a Walkman, he could walk to the beat of the music at a pace beyond what was expected for someone in his condition. Engaging the whole brain makes healing possible.

An emotional healing can come as a result of art also. How many times have you heard a song and been reminded of a favorite memory? Often that recollection can overcome feelings of depression. Movies can have the same effect. My mother explained how the movie *My Dog Skip* had touched her. The movie is a tearjerker about growing up, told through the vehicle of a boy and his dog. This movie reminded her of times when her children were young. Now that I live one thousand miles away, I only see her and Dad a few times a year. That movie reminded Mom of my childhood and helped her feel a close connection with me across the country, which lessens the hurt of being so far apart.

When the World Trade Center was hit by terrorists and fell to the ground, killing an estimated three thousand people, the world sat stunned, looking for ways to accept what had happened. In my twenty-something circle of friends, we were brought to tears. Many of us turned to television, and there found ways to cope with the pain. All of the major networks were quick to put together highly tasteful and inspiring pieces that showed the human side of this murderous tragedy. The digital storytelling didn't erase the pain for any of us, but it was the first step toward healing for much of the country.

Art can also heal broken relationships. In school, a good friend and I severed our relationship. We spent a lot of time together one summer on several youth ministry trips. Our relationship had deteriorated to the point that we were no longer speaking to each other, a situation that neither of us had any intention of changing. Then the youth ministry team put together a slide show highlighting the summer's trips. On the night that they showed those pictures, accompanied by some of my favorite Christian songs at the time, my hard heart started to melt. The artistic presentation of those memories evoked such strong emotions in both of us that we were able to look at things differently, and we reconciled immediately after the youth meeting.

. . . transcends boundaries

One of the aspects most appreciated about using art to present the Gospel is that it transcends boundaries, and it does it more effectively than nearly any other kind of strategy. Whether age, race, gender, or social class, art binds us together in ways that draw us out of our own situation. Through art we can enter into a collective experience that allows us to remove the distractions that are normally present in our daily lives. My wife is the manager at a local movie theater. She observes that most mainstream movies attract a wide variety of people. People of different cultures come together and put aside differences to experience the transforming power of narrative art.

Art allows us to get a glimpse of cultures and lifestyles other than our own. This can, in turn, give us a better appreciation and understanding for the people with whom we interact on a daily basis. For example, the film *Erin Brockovich* gives the viewer an intimate look at life as a single mother. *Boyz N the Hood* shows us life in the inner city. *Saving Private Ryan* gave the country a renewed respect for these who have fought to defend our country. I always had trouble identifying with people like Len's father who served two tours as an officer in Vietnam, but this film made the sacrifices of those in the armed forces more compelling to me.

If we want to speak to persons in a language that they can understand, diversity in the imagery, metaphors, and stories we tell will outperform any other media.

. . . reveals God

L: Art had a prominent role in the spread of early Christianity. In the late Roman Empire, as entire populations suddenly became "Christianized," vast majorities did not understand the religion of Jesus Christ and its God. Many of them, uneducated, were not capable of the abstract rhetoric that formed some early Church teaching systems. In response church leaders developed visual bases for the populace to understand the faith they were given. During this era visual representation, or iconography, became the norm for Christian teaching. Gregory the Great, pope from 590 to 604, strongly endorsed the use of the arts to reach pagan people otherwise beyond the reach of the Gospel, stating that art acted as a "Bible for the illiterate." Gregory saw art as a medium for interpreting the Christian faith to those who could not read.

Later, in the eighth century, there developed some controversy over the use of art in the Church, as some factions in the Church began to rebel against its presence. These iconoclastic tendencies were partially affected by the recent influx of Islamic practice, which emerged within the seventh century. To followers of Muhammad, pure worship was practiced without visual enticement or distraction. As Islamic influence grew culturally, their practice became increasingly identified with piety; Christians, aware of Old Testament admonishments about worshiping idols, were eager to show their own virtue. To the literate religious elite, righteousness became equated with manuscript reading rather than imagery. This was not without controversy, however; for if the visual arts did not have such power, there would not have been a great desire among the controlling powers to suppress it.[23]

In spite of their differences regarding the role of images in worship, however, most of the church at this time had one thing in common. These educated leaders in an uneducated time closely tied discipleship in a knot with education. Literacy was key to being Christian. Art was good insofar as it increased literacy. It served a distinct purpose as a tool of evangelism for a community that otherwise could not relate on a literate level. Although controversial, it acknowledged that art has value as a visual aid, or support to reading and abstract thought. Art is illustrative, or it puts imagination to abstract Christian ideas such as "Incarnation."

There is a limit, though, to the amount of instructive power that comes from eye candy. My family moved to

Texas when I was a seventh grader. At school, I was required to take a Texas history course. A football coach taught my Texas history class. He would give us regular assignments where we would open the textbook to a particular lesson and copy sections of it to paper, word for word, as a homework assignment. It was a mindless, rote practice to drill facts into our young minds. I hated it because the teacher was too lazy to do his own homework. As I look back, I realize that there was no encouragement to understand context, no nurture of the thirst for understanding. One trip to the Alamo in San Antonio gave me a better understanding of Texas history than fifty pencil push-ups.

Unfortunately, many approaches to using art and imagery in the Church are the same as in our education systems. Nicholas Negroponte observes, "With all the rage of multimedia, we have closet drill and practice believers who think they can colonize the pizzazz of a Sega game to squirt a bit more information into the minds of children."[24] With the AV mentality, often, all that extra pizzazz accomplishes, whether it is clip art in PowerPoint or ancient icons of the apostles, is an amplification of teacher haste and child passivity, or in the context of church, a preacher's pontification while the congregation sleeps. One of the goals of any learning situation is to create an environment of discovery where people can learn on their own. Don't make dazzling graphics that simply reinforce rote biblical or doctrinal or theological information. Create an environment for discovery of the truth through the use of art. Remember the Alamo.

Len Sweet describes the differences between the more Western, modern idea of knowledge—to be full of one's intellectual self and from that position offer analysis and critique—and the more biblical, Eastern (and perhaps digital) idea of knowledge: to be emptied from one's self so that revelation may occur.[25] It is not through the former, with its egotistical mental deconstructions and assumptions, but through the latter, in its humility, openness, and awareness of mystery and the unknowable, that we really find Ultimate Truth.

At least one member of the literate elite of the medieval Western church understood this. Suger, the Abbot of St.

Denis, supported art. Suger believed that, "material objects, whether natural or made by human hands, can inspire devotion, enhance meditation, and lead the soul to the experience of the transcendence."[26] To him liturgical images and objects were certainly appropriate in creating an experience of God. Suger's position paralleled a different use for the visual in church life that had been emerging in so-called Carolingian art, beginning in the eleventh century. It is primarily narrative in nature, instead of illustrative. In this mode of thought, scriptural text is considered self-sufficient in its ecclesiastical function and not aided by the presence of visual interpretation, or visual aids. In fact, applying images to scripture is the "heresy of the Greeks," because it has the potential to supersede its teaching role and become idolatrous.[27] The duty of art is to provide new texts, or different ways of approaching the Gospel, through the use of storytelling. Let preaching and reading scripture do its work, the Carolingians advocate, and allow art to do something entirely different.

Experiential and educational

These two approaches to art, as experience and as education, are married in the philosophy of Bonaventure, a thirteenth-century theologian and artist. He was a craftsman and not merely a theorist. By drawing on Pope Gregory's famous maxim, he agreed that when accompanied by preaching, images could serve as a substitute for those who could not read. He underscored his visual stance by observing male physiological behavior to prove that the visual is more stimulating than the verbal. Those who could not understand or be inspired to devotion when told might be when shown. He also believed that the visual arts helped to sustain the memory longer than the capacity afforded by aural communication.[28]

But Bonaventure's support for art had deeper roots. Beyond merely seeing it as a useful aid in teaching, he used art in his ministry because he believed that the presence of God was actually contained within his art, and not simply that art was worthwhile because of the clarity of its message. His belief reflected the biblical, Eastern view that assumes there is no spiritual world apart from the embodied tangible.

In the Christian tradition out of which Bonaventure came, art is more than a reflection or a symbol. Art is an incarnate form. It is quite radical to our symbolically trained Western minds to assume that the presence of God may be actually *in* something, and not just represented through it. But to pass something off as purely metaphor might be mistaken. While the "AV" function, or using media to support what is being communicated through other forms of preaching and teaching, is both appropriate and useful, the role of digital art has much more potential in communicating the presence of God. Throughout the ages artists and art lovers such as the Carolingians and Bonaventure have understood the power of the art form in encountering God. It is the analysts who continually have tried to rationalize, criticize, interpret, and apply meaning to every image. This sort of analysis destroys the very nature of art.

Although helpful in teaching me how to "talk church," and granting that it gave me frames for my belief systems, attending Western, modern seminary nearly took the art out of me. I remember how difficult it was after seminary when I started as full-time media minister at a church. One of my jobs was to provide graphic and video illustrations for the senior pastor's sermons on the weekends. When we first began, he would call me into his office at noon on Friday, preach his sermon to me, and then say, "Okay, now what images can I put in here?" I would try to be creative on the spot, but would draw a blank.

Over time, and even more so from a business perspective, I realized that this approach establishes a dehydrated atmosphere for matching images to ideas. Even though we use a glossy finish, we are still trying to transform lives by presenting illustrations to abstract doctrines about the Gospel: "Gee, what's a good image for grace?"

Matching images to abstract thoughts is eventually a creative dead end. Art is most powerful when it is narrative rather than ornament. Art tells stories; it doesn't make points. Certainly, good art occurs on multiple levels, and once the receiver is engaged, a deeper level of interpretation becomes a basis for meaning. I enjoy talking about a good film as much as anyone. But in order to keep me long enough to engage in discussion about a film's meaning, first the film must be a good story. It creates an experience that engages the digital age worshiper and makes them care about the characters. Out of that experience, the practices of discipleship are born.

Efrem Smith, an African-American, is deeply committed to racial reconciliation. Over the course of his first few months with me on the staff of a church, he and I had several conversations about the role of media in worship. He saw it as valuable "enhancement," or "support." I tried, in an inarticulate, frustrated manner to communicate to him that media can be much more than that.

One weekend we celebrated MLK Jr. Day with a special service devoted to racial reconciliation, and Efrem preached. We decided to have our band do a live performance of the 1980s Foreigner hit "I Want to Know What Love Is." As the band played, we projected images from the PBS Civil Rights film, *Eyes on the Prize*, across our giant screen: policemen hosing groups of blacks, turning dogs on them, throwing them in jail. One particularly disturbing scene showed an elderly African-American man trying to walk down the street. A group of young white men, more than fifteen of them, surrounded and taunted him, repeatedly knocking off his hat. Each time, he would calmly reach down and place the hat back on his head, trying to maintain his dignity as he walked down the street. Finally, as the band sang, "I want to know what love is/And I want you to show me," one youth grabbed a brick and fractured the man's skull.

Efrem looked at me during the service and said with tears in his eyes, "Now I get it." He said we could go home right then and there, because the clip preached a sermon better than anything he could say. The impact of that experience struck Efrem, and everyone in our sanctuary, deep in the gut, not because it interpreted an intellectual platform, but because it vividly displayed, in narrative form, exactly what it means to practice racial reconciliation as the body of Christ.

Worship for any age, and especially for our digital culture, is a convergence of experience and education. Doctrine without form is powerless because it doesn't engage the whole person. As Sally Morgenthaler so aptly says, "Worship is not preaching!"[29] On the other hand, form without substance is shallow and meaningless, because it is without Word. Digital age worship powerfully integrates Word with form.

> 1. Of the two approaches to art in the church, illustration and experience, which do you see more often? Think of specific examples.
> 2. Which has more impact? Again, think of specific examples. Share your view on the message board at abingdonpress.com/ebooks.

Story and expository

A writer posed the thought in *Christianity Today* magazine: "Why Christians at the turn of the 21st century should be poised on a new relationship with art is anyone's guess."[30] To observers of the postmodern phenomenon, it is not a guess at all, but rather a vivid indication of the loss of empiricism in the culture. Our digital culture finds power not in analysis but in experience, both individual and communal. To them, art is not valid so long as it didactically deconstructs some doctrinal truth. Art speaks for itself.

J: When Walter Cronkite was on CNN's *Larry King Live*, I was disappointed by Cronkite's attitude toward today's news programs. Some of his comments revealed his anachronistic roots in modern culture. When asked if he liked magazine shows he responded by saying, "I would like them better if they took the feature stories out of the daily news, the evening news, and put them on the magazine shows."

He also said, "There are so many important stories that don't get on the news at all, and instead those feature stories are run there. I cringe every time there is one of those. We ought to be hitting the news solidly for that half hour—or the twenty-three minutes after commercials and that other stuff . . . that other stuff is important. It's important to people—your health, your bank account, but put it on those magazine shows instead of those Hollywood creatures they are always showing."

Cronkite's call is to return to a modern-era way of reporting news, where the value of objectivity is forced

upon a culture of ambiguity. Contemporary news producers know that dispassionate reporting will flop. The news
is important, but if it is not told in compelling stories, then
it is no longer news to anyone. A few churches try to present the Gospel as "The Good News" in the format that
Cronkite is advocating. But the nature of reporting news
has changed, and so must the church.

   L: Moderns want facts in their bulletins, in their Bible,
and in their sermons. Facts belong in print. Postmoderns,
like myself, don't despise facts. We also want moods,
hopes, fears, imaginings, whims, speculations, night-
mares, and dreams. Postmoderns are turning away from
mainstream Christianity not because they want to pursue
mysticism or open-ended spirituality, or to make an
informed rejection of Christian doctrine. Too many postmoderns are dissatisfied with the modern trappings of
faith and its focus on objective empirical knowledge.
Modernity kills wonder and mystery in the name of science. There's a vacuum that liturgy once filled in the culture that's been stripped away, and seekers in our culture
are looking for ways to replace it. As a result, many people who grew up in liturgical denominations go to "contemporary churches" but end up expressing general dis-
satisfaction with what they call its "shallowness." They
say, "Well, maybe a hymn now and then is a good thing."
What drives this confusion? I believe it's because they're
looking for some sense of mystery and wonder that good
liturgy provided to previous generations. Through art on
the screen, digital age worship needs to recapture the
emotive power of the wonder and awe of God and the
majesty of creation. This awe does not have as much to do
with "traditional" versus "contemporary" worship as
most church leaders think. This sense of holy has more to
do with a sense of discovery that we felt the first time we
saw the ocean as a child.
   The screen is not the best place for facts; its function is
not to illustrate factual truth. The screen's function in digital age worship is to approach emotional truth. This emotive power is different from emotionalism, which is an
enthusiastic state of fervor that some religious persons

expect during intimacy with God. Emotive perception is a different way of encountering God. Jesus says in the Gospel of Matthew that there are three ways that we may love God: heart, soul, and mind. Moderns get an "A" for loving God with the mind. Postmoderns focus on the screen because it lends itself to the second and third ways: through the heart, and especially within the soul. This heart-and-soul communion with God occurs primarily in stories.

J: Ingrid's five-year-old daughter, Madeline, cannot end her night without a story. I recall one night when Madeline insisted that I read her "The Bernstein Bears Go on Vacation." I did my best Mama and Papa bear voices, and although I was self-impressed with dazzling special voice effects, she wasn't. "Read it like Mom and Dad, Jason," she said. I continued to read the story to her, this time in my "normal" voice. As I got into the story I realized it was getting late. I decided that I'd give her the "Cliff Notes" version of this book, without asking her permission. As I would skip a line or change a word, she knew. She would promptly recite the correct words for me in a tone that made me wonder who was really in control of the situation. At that time she couldn't read a word, but she knew the story so well, that any change or omission was immediately brought to my attention.

Media theorist George Gerbner says that stories are the seamless web of our culture.[31] Stories become so real we base our playtime and even our real time on them. We as Christians have the opportunity to (pardon the cliché) tell the greatest story ever told. Creative story-based imagery can make the stories of the Bible come alive and touch us at a heart level. The method we use to tell the Gospel stories can either run off or reach those we're trying to reach. Making the jump from an informational approach to an inspirational approach can unleash the creative power of the God of the Bible on the Church.

L: However, in order for the stories of the Bible to be transforming, first they must be told. Has it ever struck you how little the Bible is present in worship today? Most of the time, Protestant worship is expository. In the past, worship contained both the telling of the biblical story itself, and a commentary on it. Now, we almost always get the commentary. Sermon-centered worship, if based on the Bible at all, is mostly the presentation of one person's understanding of biblical stories; based on his or her private, quiet analysis of Biblical text.

A contemporary church in a large urban area had about seven thousand in worship the Sunday I went, and their technical capabilities for worship were impressive. Their worship service that weekend was "The Perfect Storm." They used the storm metaphor as a symbol of the distractions that obstruct us from listening to God. They had a fifteen-second animation to bridge the feature song to the sermon of a storm cloud with a lightning bolt. Even though it was entirely ornamental, hung from 3-points and a salvation call, the digital media was the best I had ever seen. As technically impressed as I was, though, I summarized my experience with the thought that excellence, without integration, an artistic touch, or a visual parable, misses the deepest power of art for our digital culture.

A pastor's approach, or an entire church's approach, to digital media is all in how he, she, or they understand Scripture. The Bible is not an instructional manual for life, an enhanced version of the Torah. The Bible is a rich, inspired heritage of stories of God's movement of love in, to, and through the created people of this world. Debates about the Bible as either fallible or inspired, metaphorical or literal, treat the New Testament as something to be analyzed and written about. If God wanted us to debate more Laws, the Cross would be unnecessary. Religion for puzzle lovers? Of course not. Christ is the fulfillment of the Law. Faith in Jesus is not about more rules; especially obscure ones that require decoder books, such as the *Genesis Code*. Faith in Jesus is about relationship, and the best way to understand that relationship is through the telling and retelling of stories.

The Gospels are full of incredible stories of what it is like to hang out with Jesus. Those stupid questions the disciples are always asking are the same stupid questions *we'd* ask![32] In addition to Jesus stories, stories of the early church in the remainder of the New Testament give us understanding for the realities of church now. Stories from throughout Christian history help us to find the common struggles of humankind trying to live up to the grace that has been given to us. Stories from last week have the immediacy of the present. However, each of these stories must be told in ways that people of the digital culture can understand. That is why art *for this present digital culture* is so vitally important.

J: A digital storyteller finds ways to relate the Gospel to digital culture. Here are a few examples:

"Good to Go?" tells the story of an astronaut's journey into space. If you look closely at the left part of the image you'll see the astronaut preparing for his journey as he walks down the hall with his equipment in hand. In the middle, you see him waving to the spectators who are gathered to watch his historical departure into space. On the right the rocket lifts off toward the moon, and finally, just to the left of the rocket, you see him standing on the moon.

"Good to Go?" retells Peter's story in John 21:1-19. After Jesus' crucifixion, Peter returns to his life as a fisherman. The resurrected Jesus returns to him with a dramatic question: Do you return to your old life or do you follow Christ into a new life? Are you "good to go"? Leaving all that is comfortable on earth represents the monumental decision that Peter makes regarding leaving his town, his job, and even his family, to fulfill his calling from Christ. **(Experience "Good to Go" Chapter 15 on the DVD.)**

"Ultimate love" simply repaints an image of a familiar biblical story. Of course, this is Mary washing Jesus' feet. Whether the story is presented orally or not, the image is more potent than words. Sometimes literal visual interpretations of Scripture can make viewers feel a bit disconnected, but in this case we felt that the image of Mary's act of love could be presented in its original setting and still connect to our culture. Digital culture is not opposed to tradition; it represents it in fresh ways, through new media.

"Messy Love" tells the story of a mother's love for her child. No matter how frustrated a mother gets with her children, she still is willing to change dirty diapers, clean up messes, and wash feet. This retelling is our take on what Jesus might have felt for his disciples when he washed their feet: unconditional love to ones who can only take and cannot give in return.

L: The art both reveals the power of the experience of the story, of being "in" it, and also provides expository openings, or doors to learning through the story and applying it to our own lives. They contain experience and education. A strong theology of art for the digital culture church must contain both.

Digital mindshift

For worship, digital art will take on new forms for the telling of our faith's stories. It will begin with true stories of our faith, grounded in Scripture, and will present them as Jesus did, in the form of a visual parable. A short video clip. A live reading accompanied by music and a series of graphics. A segment from a film. All woven together to communicate a single, central theme, based as Jesus' parables on the deep human needs of the people in the streets, who have come for an experience of God.

One of our productions is of a century-old steam train pulling into a depot. By using only facial expressions, we attempted to communicate the anticipation, excitement, and fear of the passengers-to-be as they waited for the train to take them someplace they had never been, in a time when train travel meant movement into a whole new world. Such was the feeling of people contemplating the cost of following Jesus in Luke 9:51-62. The key moment in the video is a close-up of the

conductor yelling, "All aboard!" Jesus calls us to forget about burying the dead, get on board and immediately follow him, because the train is leaving the station. **(Experience "All Aboard" Chapter 09 on the DVD.)**

This clip, combined with the song "People Get Ready (There's a Train a'comin')"— covered in the 1980s by Rod Stewart—and a call to worship tying the theme and the scripture together, sets a strong tone for worship by creating a vivid experience of the immediacy of following Jesus.

One pastor wrote in an e-mail that she is worried about the use of images distracting from the spoken word. I encouraged her to reconsider her understanding of what digital media is. I reminded her that the Word of God in the Bible is not limited to a specific medium. I told her to begin to ask herself and others around her, "How can we produce digital art that communicates the Word of God?" I also told her, "Think of it as an equally important, entirely different medium from oral speech and print. When does speaking distract from the power of the visual experience?"

She replied, "Well, what about losing the Bible in the art?" The story of Jesus is more real, not less, because it parallels the myths of Osiris and Balder. In God's desire to reach humanity, God chose to encompass the myth. The writer says, "Just as Christ came not to abolish the Law but to fulfill it, so he came not to put an end to myth but to take all that is most essential in the myth up into himself and make it real."[33] Art doesn't swallow the Bible. It makes it more real.

Perhaps a story that is passed through multiple media across entire generations, over centuries of time, may need to be reconstructed to get its full impact. There was much controversy a few years ago when the decision was made to restore the Sistine Chapel. Art historians claimed that Michelangelo created these dark images as a reflection of the social and theological themes of his day. But the restoration process cleansed these theories by revealing a vibrant, colorful reproduction of the stories of the Bible.

Verbatim integrity is not the key to unlocking the power of stories buried in Scripture. Instead, good exegesis of the Bible opens up a world of creative imaginings where dynamic equivalents can demonstrate scriptural truth and apply it to contemporary culture. So don't be so literal. Instead, find ways to capture the essence of the biblical story.

Another of our productions captures the horror and healing of the demons and the pigs story in Luke 8:26-39. Like the man possessed with demons, we all are affected by forces of evil that manifest themselves in such things as the inability to control our impulses and the tendency toward addictive behavior, which lead to family dysfunction and damaged relationships. These forces are like termites, especially in the clay-like Texas soil where I live. It is said in Texas that either you have termites, or you're going to get them. And when you treat them, you never

really kill them; you only transfer them to your neighbor's yard. Termites are creepy and crawly. They give people the hee-bie-jeebies. So we produced an animation of a colony of termites feasting that get ousted by a big dose of termite spray, and the words "Get Out!" It's gross! But it really captures the experience.

This is the latter of the two approaches, interpretation and experience. While termites metaphorically represent demons on many levels, it is not necessary for the metaphor to *exactly* capture every nuance of the demons and the pigs story. The first and primary purpose of the termites is not to function as the interpretation of the story. It is to create an *experience* of the story. In the experience, having many interpretive parallels or sub-roots is a wonderful bonus to the basic root metaphor.

Developing expressions of faith can come through avenues beyond the exercise of our cerebrums. Good art in any form, whether sculpture, novels, or films, has the potential to act as a transformative medium for us, because it engages the mystery that is God's presence in our lives. Let us not reduce everything God has created and does to a mental exercise, and say that what is engaging is entertaining and therefore evil. Let us acknowledge that Christian worship, has a long tradition of what some would call "entertainment." And let us allow God to use our God-given creativity to push the culture toward an experience of God through its own media.

Creating an experience of the story involves more than simply a video clip, however. Digital age experiences make a canvas of the entire worship space. In the next chapter we will look at creating liturgy that draws upon, and redeems, the cultural language of the digital age.

20. The full sermon, by Dr. Frank Thomas, is available on-line at http://www.ginghamsburg.org/.

21. Jerry Solomon and Jimmy Williams, "Art and the Christian." http://www.probe.org/docs/artandxn.html.

22. These animations, called "Reconciliation," may be found on *The Wired Church* (Nashville: Abingdon, 1999) CD-ROM.

23. John Dillenberger, *A Theology of Artistic Sensibilities: The Visual Arts and the Church* (New York: Crossroad, 1986), p. 57. Dillenberger cites similar patterns in medieval and reformed iconoclasm, suggesting that the suppression of objects, which led to idolatry, only brought out other destructive powers.

24. Negroponte, *Being Digital*, p. 199.

25. Leonard Sweet, *Post-Modern Pilgrims: First Century Passion for the 21st Century Church* (Nashville: Broadman and Holman, 2000), pp. 145-46.

26. As quoted in Gregor Goethals, *The Electronic Golden Calf: Images, Religion, and the Making of Meaning.* (Cambridge: Cowley, 1990.) p. 24.

27. Dillenberger, *A Theology of Artistic Sensibilities*, pp. 36-38.

28. Ibid, p. 43.

29. Sally Morgethaler, *Worship Evangelism* (Grand Rapids: Zondervan, 1999), p. 43.

30. "The Wright Stuff," by Lauren F. Winner, *Christianity Today*, April 23, 2001, p. 87.

31. As quoted in *The Wired Church*, p. 25.

32. Tom Boomershine, *Story Journey* (Nashville: Abingdon, 1989). Through practical examples in the Gospels, Tom gives framework to a narrative approach to faith.

33. Markos, p. 36.

Chapter 4
Erasing Boundaries

J: A man lay beaten on the ground, desperate for the help of those who would pass by him. The priest and the Levite, two God-followers, were both unwilling to help the man because they were strictly adhering to boundaries that had been created to "protect" their religious traditions. The Samaritan, while not a God-follower, had compassion for the man in his predicament, and in his act of kindness erased the many boundaries that stood between the two.

The seekers outside the doors of your church are lying by the side of the road, hurting. They seek good news and healing. Are we willing to cross, sometimes erase, the boundaries that exist between the church and those who are disconnected from it?

The church builds solid boundaries to preserve incomprehensible traditions, high culture, worn-out hierarchies, and classic (read: class) architecture. With the emerging digital culture speaking with a louder voice than ever, progressive churches are scrambling to use digital art forms as the key to erasing the boundaries that exist between church, secular, folk, pop, and high cultures. As each slat of the fence is erased the church gets closer to reaching the world. The results of these efforts will allow us to form a whole new Christ-centered community of digital culture.

Culture and technology

L: A pastor expressed his intention to preach about Zacchaeus. In searching for screen images to support his sermon, he asked us, "Are there any famous *masterworks* related to Zacchaeus that I could use?"

J: His statement assumed a very specific artistic style. I loved to paint with oils in college, but the majority of people in digital culture expect a very different style.

L: It is not enough to simply talk about art in general terms, because the word *art* means very different things to different people. Every culture has its own distinctive examples of art, including the emerging digital culture. This is because every time and space has evolving technology. In fact, technology is such a powerful force that a social approach to it goes a long way in defining its legacy.[34]

Ancient history is even commonly defined according to the technology of its various periods, for example the Stone Age, the Iron Age, and the Bronze Age. In each of these ages, the primary technology is the primary medium for art. For example, cave paintings show both instruments and canvases that were a part of that era's technology. The same is true in the modern era. The popularity of the novel (and the Bible) correlates with the ubiquity of mass-print culture. In every era, art and technology are intermingled. That is why we are now living in a digital culture, not simply a postmodern culture.

J: Even what we now call "classic" art, the very *masterworks* that the pastor mentioned, were created to speak to indigenous culture. The Stone Age brought about primitive images carved with bone and rock, which were used to tell the stories of the day. In the Bronze and Iron Ages artists became experts in the metallurgical arts. The art became more sophisticated and so did the culture. In Egypt, hieroglyphics were used not only to inscribe sacred texts, but also to express sound and ideas through vivid colors and pictures. These artistic renderings were held in high regard by the people of that day. Michelangelo was commissioned to create reflections of God with the tools of the Renaissance. These tools brought about new energy and raised the bar for what was possible. And now centuries later the tools have evolved yet again. Shouldn't we then use our digital technology to create *masterworks* that speak to our generation just as the artists who came before us?

L: As we collectively enter the digital world, we are faced with three primary cultures, all defined according to their position in relationship to the main technology of the past five hundred years: print by mass, mechanized production. These primary, known cultures of modernism in the West are *high, pop,* and *folk*.

High culture refers to the legacy of European money. Until approximately fifty years ago, high culture controlled mass, mechanized media production, and with it they controlled society.

Pop culture is the culture of the mainstream, middle-class Western world. In the latter half of the twentieth century, primarily because of the rise of television, popular culture gained the upper hand (and ever since, high culturati have been moaning about the "dumbing down" of the world).

Folk culture, on the other hand, is a grouping of an entire series of small, ethnic cultures that historically didn't fit into the European mainstream. In the past generation, diversity issues have significantly broadened folk culture's presence in the mainstream, to the point where segments of folk culture have integrated with pop culture (e.g., hip-hop).

Whereas the mainstream culture of the digital age blurs these boundaries, the church elite remains strictly tied to modern-era technology. Throughout the modern era, the "mainline" Protestant church sat squarely in high culture. In many "Sunday-morning churches" (a term used by Lyle Schaller in *The Seven-Day-a-Week Church*), worship is an expression of high-culture sensibility, from four-part chorales to silent reading of Scripture. Though it would tolerate the other two cultures for the sake of "mission," rarely, if ever, has the established high-culture church leadership been willing to alter or sacrifice their dominant cultural identity for the sake of the Gospel. Tom Boomershine calls this the sacralization of media, defined as making certain technologies more holy than others.[35] However, along with the secular culture, in the past generation the church has embraced folk culture out of a greater sensitivity to issues of racial inclusion. For example, The United Methodist Church celebrates Martin Luther King Jr. Sunday and Native American Sunday every year.

Popular culture, however, is still not widely accepted. To the modern church, pop culture is considered a subculture: shallow, carnal, and worst of all, illiterate. Though it may seem amazing to the digerati, one sometimes hears high culture leaders brag about not owning a television.

New symbols for ancient truths

As modernism fades and digital culture emerges, many churches are trying to revive the high-culture idea of what is commonly called "fine art," or the art of high, modern culture. Several prominent Christian publications observe a "renaissance of the arts" in the Church. This is probably a natural first response to the sudden technical opportunities many churches have in worship, because what is known as "fine art" is such a vivid, recognized model in the Church's recent history.

Though the Church is largely divorced from the art world now, it is most comfortable with the art of high culture. Fine art, or art for the "cultured" (including such mediums as orchestral music from more than one hundred years ago, sculpture, and oil painting), is an artifact of the enlightenment. Many large, Protestant downtown churches have parlors and art galleries that attempt to take on the same appearance as the local fine art museum.

J: When church leaders decide to incorporate media into worship, they first look to reproductions of fine art. In pursuit of this form, they often attempt to stuff too much artistic meaning into a piece, sailing over the heads of the congregations they're trying to reach. The basic problem with exclusively using fine art is that the majority of a congregation is illiterate concerning famous paintings and composers. Classic fine art can be somewhat abstract to the average person sitting in the pew.

We like to attend independent film festivals. Many of the pieces shown there are very "artsy." We often find ourselves scratching our heads, wondering when the various films will finish. Some of the filmmakers are trying so hard to "make art" that they lose much of their audience along the way. The abstract nature of these pieces may be so esoteric that for the most part only those involved with the production would know how to properly interpret them. Some of the other films are created in more of a pop art style. We seem to discuss more freely after seeing a film created in a pop art style.

L: To many churches, art of the popular culture is not acceptable. This elitist attitude has roots that go deeper than the rise of modernism and mass printing. The social and religious chasm set in the pre–Middle Ages widened as generations passed between the educated minority and the illiterate majority. Literates debated over the role of art, while out in the streets, popular piety was almost entirely visual. The visual was the system of spirituality for the common people, while it was merely a secondary, supplemental teaching tool for the literate. The two strands ran on parallel tracks: the poorer, illiterate, and less powerful cultural majority has a visual faith, while the richer, literate, and more powerful cultural minority bases their faith on manuscripts. These literate leaders meant well when taking up the ministry of tutoring the illiterate, insisting that a better life could be had with more education. But others missed the point by insisting that the illiterate take on culturally conditioned systems of literacy in order to practice true faith.

In the face of the iconoclastic influence of the Reformers during the cultural renaissance of the fifteenth and sixteenth centuries, the Catholic Church slowly began to reappropriate art. But it was limited to the expression of the educated and powerful upper class. Bach was a staff musician at a cathedral in Germany for much of his career. Michelangelo's greatest works were contract jobs for the Vatican.

However, in spite of their high-culture commissions, these works of "fine art" revealed God in their time and bridged divides to the lower and middle classes because they used what were then current, popular imagery and conventions to reveal the human condition. For example, Renaissance Italian paintings that graphically focused on the bleeding body of Christ, such as the works of Rembrandt, revealed a God who was immanently present to an Italian culture, who for a millennia had primarily understood Jesus as more divine than human.

The same painting communicates a very different message today. Twenty-first-century American culture, with its focus on sexuality in commerce, sees the human body very differently from fifteenth-century Italian culture. Just because it pointed to God then doesn't mean it will now. In fact, most art from previous cultures has an opposite effect in our world today. Rather than drawing its original receivers out from their limited worldviews, art from previous cultures now draws us as students into the culture in which it was made. Rather than pointing away from its created culture, it primarily points to itself. Ditto for much of our sacred music traditions in the church.

J: Fine art is a language of its own. In and of itself, it can be hard to understand for the nonexpert. If we apply it, and other potentially confusing languages to the Gospel, we force worshipers to wade through the interpretation of both the artistic language and religious language. Using art to communicate the Gospel is supposed to make it easier to understand, not harder.

L: In one worship service we decided to feature prominently the creation section of Michelangelo's Sistine Chapel, the Adam on a cloud touching fingers with God. The first two of our four weekend services went fine, but just before the start of the third service, one of the staff members came bounding up the steps to our control room loft. "Cover up that private part!" Of course, Adam is lying on the cloud, nude. So, we quickly opened Photoshop and painted a quarter-inch cube of solid color to cover Adam's weensy private part in the image. Though I viewed the entire painting as art, others did not. Instead they saw a potentially pornographic image that has no place in worship. And he was right: We live in a world in which the human body has been perverted through pornography. This particular art didn't point to the immanence of the God of the New Testament. When art points to itself or to any human creator—Look, I did this!—the congregation is misled.

Amazingly, even as old-guard churches age and evaporate, the majority of its leaders, educated in seminaries, still look with disdain on the contemporary expressions of popular culture. While there is certainly nothing wrong with fine art mediums, most people don't consider themselves really into "fine art." To the average person I know, the word *art* refers to what hangs in a museum. Appreciation and involvement in this type of art are a hobby, or a subculture, but not something that involves seekers. This doesn't mean that the dominant culture lacks art. Rather, pop art is everywhere, and most of us partake of it all the time.

Though images, symbols, and metaphors may evoke power in any cultural context, when they become familiar, they lose their power and take on a codified form much like the idols of ancient days. We have seen depictions of the cross so often in worship that our hearts have forgotten the power of the Passion story. For many people, instead of a reference to the shocking tale of Jesus' redemption, the cross has become a codified sacred symbol for worship space. A church in the Midwest, and thousands like it, faces a problem of where to put their screen. There is only one logical place to put it, but a massive cross occupies the space. They solved the problem, and appeased all parties, by placing the screen over the cross and then, when it wasn't being used for something else, placing a seamless picture of the covered, up portion of the cross on the screen. It had the effect of making the screen look completely transparent. Their solution is indicative of how codified and sacralized the cross has become: It is anathema to cover the wooden sculpted cross, in spite of the fact the medium of the screen can show crosses in much more dynamic, awakened fashion.

Images (and metaphors) die, particularly when they lose their power to shock us into seeing things a new way. Christianity is piled high with the carcasses of old images and metaphors that now lack the provocative power to give life to our faith, from the ChiRho to "Pass It On." Media of any form or age has a shelf life beyond which it is necessary to either reintroduce or create new expressions for our faith.

Artists bring new life to traditional symbols and ideas, whether it is through recasting the ancient metaphors in new ways or inventing new ways of entering into ancient ideas.

Some people say that art is timeless! Indeed, some art may be rather timeless. Some art is so powerful it transcends the generation, the culture, even the era in which it is made. But even the most powerful image can lose its power over time. As moving as the Sistine Chapel is now, imagine what it was like to the world in which it debuted. Eventually, even the most powerful art subsides as the civilization subsides in which it was made. As old as the Sistine Chapel is, we still live in the emerging Western world in which it was made. Michelangelo worked with the same perspective that our current eyes expect. Do we collectively look at any pre-perspective artwork the same way?

My colleague has a beautiful icon in his house. It is a religious artifact from the Byzantine Empire of the Middle Ages. It shows the Madonna and Christ child. They are flat, with circle halos over their heads. Its halos, its ornate gold treatment, its texture all point to the world in which it was made, and to a particular theology. But this piece of art wasn't created for our critical analysis; it was created for religious edification for a very different world from the one in which we live today.

We are in no way advocating the abandonment of tradition. The challenge we have as producers for the digital age is to take edification from the art of previous ages and rejuvenate it on a new canvas.

J: You might think we're disrespectful, perhaps thinking that there is a large generation gap, or that we have not lived long enough. We know that for many these established forms and images are very meaningful. Although images have a life span, it is possible to recast them in new and reinvigorating ways. The Walk to Emmaus/Chrysalis weekends, sponsored by The United Methodist Church, provide a great example. These weekends have been extremely effective in recasting some of the more traditional images. The Chrysalis retreat, for example, is sprinkled with a great mix of traditional and digital age components. From the music, to the message, to the interactive nature of the table discussions, symbols have been recast. The reason some of these symbols and images work is that they are tied closely to experience.

The gap is not so much between the generations as it is between the insiders and the outsiders. Images that speak to someone who has been part of the Church since birth are very different from those that speak to someone who has not yet entered the Church. Pastors already know that they are to be students of the culture where they live. What are the new symbols that can reach this generation with the message of Christ?

L: Stained glass is a prime example of the life cycle of symbols and forms. Beginning in the Gothic period of the middle to late twelfth century, stained glass became a dominant artistic medium in churches because it was relatively noncontroversial. To pro-image leaders, it is image-based and therefore acceptable; to anti-image leaders, it is non-threatening because of its dependency on something outside itself for completion: that is, the light shining in from behind it. Stained glass was both aesthetically pleasing and served an interpretive function, in the education of the church community. Further, it is relatively free from idolatry, veneration, and worship. Such art is both meditative to the general public and appropriately subservient to literate preferences of the written word. Thus, it became an institution and lasted through immense cultural change. But in the modern age, when abstract thought replaced stories in worship, stained glass moved from telling the Gospel through stories to . . . well, ornament. Thousands of mainline churches, built in the Colonial style, contain windows of simple panes of glass, lightly tinted various shades of blue, purple, green, yellow, and clear. The iconoclastic glass of these churches is completely disconnected from the culture (and those inside), vague and meaningless.

Stained glass no longer serves the powerful role that it once did in the life of the Church. The screen, and to a larger degree the entire canvas of the worship space, has the potential to be the stained glass, and more so, for digital culture.

J: Although stained glass may have been reduced to abstract shapes in some of our newest buildings, it was once a crucial technology for the Gospel presentation. We'd like to see leaders return to the stained-glass methodology of teaching. Long ago those images breathed life into the messages shared from the pulpit. Now with the screen, the glass can be changed from week to week. What once took highly skilled craftsmen months to produce can be done by the artist of today in a fraction of the time. The bonus is that today's stained glass can tell multiple stories. The images can move, the colors can change, and the renderings can again reach the culture in a form that is reflective of the time in which we live.

Redeeming pop culture

L: One of the rebuttals that we often hear (mainly from what some pastors call the "old saints" and others call the "blue hairs") is that popular culture in all of its profanity is incapable of the artistic power of "fine art." Implicit is the belief that popular culture never made the world a better place. Consider the list of the most influential pop songs of the twentieth century, which were aired during a TV special. Near the top of the list was "Superstition," by Stevie Wonder. In between original footage of Stevie bobbing and weaving in front of a synthesizer, I saw sound bites of weathered old cats telling how, when Stevie played his new song, all of a sudden, white kids in the suburbs were being seen with black kids, all grooving together to Stevie's beat.

As I watched, I began to mentally list the pop cultural moments in our American history that had a profound impact on race relations. From Stevie Wonder to Jackie Robinson to Bill Cosby, which had the most effect on changing the hearts of America about race? "Cultured" art? Legislation? From my viewpoint, the biggest difference is that the late twentieth-century had a mass media fueled pop culture. Run-DMC jamming on "Walk This Way" with Aerosmith on MTV in the mid-1980s did more to improve race relations with my peers than legislation or fine art ever did. Pop culture. Pop art.

It amazes and puzzles me when people look with disdain on pop culture. Exactly what makes "fine art," or the art of high culture, better? Because it is the preference of the educated, wealthy, and powerful? Is this how Jesus would prefer we conduct ourselves and do our ministry? Or is it because high culture is more full of educated, compassionate, enlightened people who have a better understanding of what the Gospels truly are about? One often sees more selfless compassion among lower socioeconomic persons than among the egocentric elite.

I would rather worship a God who is alive in the forms of expression present in today's pop culture. For those who say these forms of expression are shallow, remember the words of C. S. Lewis: "A live dog is better than a dead lion." When designing worship, the question need not be, Is it appropriate, but rather, Is it alive?

As important as it is to acknowledge and capitalize on popular cultural expression, the church must do more than just imitate. Worship must rise above the culture(s) in which it resides and to which it refers. Lord knows we've seen enough *Survivor* and *Who Wants to Be a Millionaire* send-ups in worship all over North America that betray the church by the values advertised on those shows. Merely referencing, or more accurately ripping off, culture is not only meaningless, it's dangerous, because it rips away the very thing that a seeking world comes to church for in the first place.

J: When churches present a *Who Wants to Be a Millionaire* drama, they should ask, Did anyone know what it was about? Do they remember the biblical truth connected to it? Was there any? These are important questions to ask about a piece when using cultural references such as *Survivor, Millionaire, Saturday Night Live,* and nearly any other cultural phenomenon. Are you redeeming the culture when you parody it or its style, or simply ripping it off? "Who Wants to go to Heaven?"; "Who wants to be a Gazillionaire?"; and the most clever of all, "Who Wants to be a Church-onaire?" I don't have a clue how any of these gimmicks connected to scripture.

This rip-off trap is a short cut. I must confess my guilt. I played Regis in a *Millionaire* drama that was a lifeline short of being redeemed. We worked hard to put it together, and it was done with extreme excellence, but even as a key player, I could not tell you now what the point was. I'm not sure I could have told you then. Many of this culture's most popular shows are often horrid when it comes to values. *Millionaire* is about greed. *Survivor* is about treachery. The bad guy wins.

With mistakes behind us, we learn how to redeem culture. One story, presented at Ginghamsburg, was from John, where Jesus curses the fig tree. We felt then that the original metaphor of fruit, vines, and branches would still connect somewhat with this culture, but we gave it an extra push by sharing the story through the eyes of the freshly popular Crocodile Hunter. Viewers would identify it both by scripture reference and metaphor. We have shown that piece sev-

eral times at conferences and often we ask the crowd for the biblical metaphor, and it never fails that several will always yell out, "Vine and the branches." If we can balance cultural references and biblical messages we will be successful at reaching the world we currently live in. **(Experience "The Crocodile Hunter," Chapter 17 on the DVD.)**

L: A seminary professor told me of a student who wanted to use a film clip for a class project that showed Jesus cursing and flipping the finger, which deeply offended the professor. As I listened to his story, it occurred to me that in all probability his student wasn't attracted by the clip because she found it offensive, or shocking for its own sake, but rather found something in it that reflected to her Jesus' humanity. She probably wasn't agnostic, but rather ignostic.[36]

It is not our job as ministers to bring the church into the world, but rather through exposing the church to the world, lift the world out of its own mire. If a worshiper leaves the spectacle of experiential, digital age worship with only the memory of a pop culture reference, then that worship has stumbled. The purpose of such a reference, or a metaphor or story or experience of any kind, is to draw people into an experience of God. The worshipper should reenter their workaday world, bump into that reference, and be reminded of God's ongoing presence in their lives, not that their church did a cheesy counterfeit of it. The world comes to church not for second-rate imitations, but for an experience of God, which is only possible if it is something *that they can understand*.

Another complaint that we hear (mainly from the digital and largely absent under–thirty audience) is that "contemporary worship" is a feeble re-creation of what was once pop culture. One of the biggest challenges is to continue to find ways to redeem current cultural expression. Each generation tends to make their particular forms and styles holy. This is a natural reaction. Most of us tend to confuse Christ and the horse he rode into our lives, so to speak. I'm fairly young, but as I progressively get older and potentially more separated from dominant cultural expression, I will find it increasingly difficult to avoid falling into a comfortable pattern of creating worship that works for me, and not for the world.

Digital liturgy

Part of the struggle that comes in learning to communicate in digital language is that there are so few examples. Historically, the model for Christian worship has come in the forms and rituals of liturgy. The word *liturgy,* while long-since reified to mean boring, traditional worship, actually connotes a specific ordering of worship that creates a unified experience. Good liturgy is thematic. Good worship for digital culture creates a liturgical whole from the sums of its media matrix.

By using old wineskins, the modern high-culture church is vainly trying to generate enthusiasm for dying or dead liturgy through the use of digital technology, but these efforts amount to little more than life support if they are based in words rather than images. On the other hand, many contemporary churches are eager to embrace digital technology but cannot see past using it as enhancement for resisting the intellectual encroachment of modernism. For example, Sally Morgenthaler describes the music portion of contemporary church worship as a random collection of hit praise songs strung together and sung at a fast pace, which reminds her of worship "with a gun to your head."[37] Missing is a sense of transcendence and meditation.

The emerging digital culture requires a new form for worship. Acute changes in technology so thoroughly disassemble established constructs that it is impossible to regroup and do the same thing, but just on a screen. A basic rule for churches that begin to think about digital cultures: *Radical changes in technology beget radical changes in expression.* When we insist upon "digital culture" in this book and DVD, we are observing a completely new wineskin, with new forms of expression.

J: The media melting pot of digital age culture reflects art from many sources. Postmodern generations combine many different genres and styles together to form an entirely new style. For example, in the world of fashion, it is not uncommon to see clothing from the '70s, '80s, and '90s combined into a new category. Len and I shot a 1970s-style video and sought authentic clothing to match. We located a small shop that was filled with the fashions of the past. In the twenty minutes that we were hunting down our costumes we saw an incredible amount of traffic. These dingy relics from the past were sought as if they were the newest summer line from Nike. **(See "Street Talk: What do you hope for?" Chapter 03 on the DVD.)**

The same is true for music. After spending an afternoon looking for a definition of *Ska* on the web, I've found that there is no clear consensus on exactly what it is. It originated in Jamaica in the 1960s, has heavily evolved, and combines jazz, blues, and punk rock. It is marked by its use of horns, fast-tempo drums, and strongly emphasized offbeat. Kids love it. This has been called "ancient future," or forming a new style that draws from the best of many different worlds, both ancient and contemporary.

In the 1950s artists such as Andy Warhol attempted to fuse elements of popular and high culture to erase boundaries between the two. His art provided a common ground where high-culture artists and laypeople could come to terms with art together. He wanted art to reach people where they were and realized that most of our society does not live in high culture. His approach was to use common imagery found in comic strips, Coke bottles, and soup cans to express artistic ideas.

L: Art of any culture does not create people of that culture. Its purpose is not to perpetuate any particular belief system or socioeconomic worldview. Its purpose, in whatever form it is created, is to illuminate the human condition, regardless of cultural category. To transcend our own boundaries, the church needs to purge itself of the elitism of high culture that prevents so many people from experiencing the Gospel of Jesus. Good art uses the latest technological advances to move beyond whatever cultural context in which it is born. Like Michelangelo inventing new techniques in his Sistine Chapel project, and Shakespeare hanging out at the press, we can use the latest in digital technology to create masterworks that speak to all cultures.

So far, digital culture seems to continually redefine itself. Pursuit of ministry in digital culture means constantly analyzing the usefulness of any symbol in communicating the power of the Gospel. It takes a lot of work! The last time I checked, God never called us to rest on our laurels.

Digital culture is not a single culture, but it's a composite, a mix and match of a number of cultures, all thrown together in our age of inclusion to create a single new whole. It's sort of like a melting pot, except it isn't. Instead, it's a celebration of variety in which each piece retains its own identity, while forming a new synthesis.

34. Susan White, *Christian Worship and Technological Change* (Nashville: Abingdon, 1994).
35. From an unpublished book by Thomas Boomershine, forthcoming from Fortress Press.
36. "Ignostic" is a term coined by George Hunter, in *How To Reach Secular People* (Nashville: Abingdon, 1992).
37. Sally Morgenthaler, *Worship Evangelism* (Grand Rapids: Zondervan, 1999).

Chapter 5
Digital Age Worship

L: One of the first things that turned me on to the Bible when I was a teenager was the discovery that in parts it read as a good tale. I remember being a freshman in college and sitting up late in my dorm room poring through the New Testament as if I were reading a great novel. I especially loved Luke and Acts, and the ways in which the writer wrote a strong narrative. This new appreciation was counter to the perception that I had of the Bible while growing up. My parents had encouraged me to read the Bible on a regular basis, and had even given me a plan to do so, but until college I couldn't move past the Sunday school impression, as an adolescent, that it was merely the world's thickest rulebook for living.

During graduate school and then seminary, my experience matured into the realization that the Bible could be experienced as communication similar to a novel, radio show, or movie. In Scripture, of course, are many ways in which writers communicate the Word, and there are many types of narrative that communicate the Word.

Communicating the Word through digital technology

In some of our churches the Word of God is confused with the written word. The Word is different from the word. The Gospel of John tells us that the Word is eternal, which means it is not contained within a particular communication system. This means that no single communication system is more holy than another. Some disagree out of reverence for the printed page, which was at first an astonishing and rare technology. Others agree in theory but disagree in practice, for they have not analyzed the consequences of such a statement. A worship practitioner's approach to the various media systems is profoundly guided by his or her approach to these relative degrees of holiness for multiple media.

Media guru Marshall McLuhan uttered during the 1960s the infamous dictum that "the medium is the message." Christian adherents to this view suggest that the Word must be told from the preferred communication systems that were tested throughout church history, because other systems alter its meaning in the minds of the hearers. As well-established communication and educational theory developed on paper during the golden years of broadcast television, we were all bound to become slaves to the boob tube, Big Brother, and corporate marketing interests.

More recent communication studies show that a mix of media is more powerful than any single form. For example, regardless of the violent or sexual messages on the television screen, an active parent deconstructing those messages is a more powerful force in the hearts and minds of their children. Mass media has the potential to be a cultural forum, a means of interaction and education. Children of the digital age, however, are taking the TV screen a step further. Don Tapscott points out that the "N-Generation" of teenagers would rather participate in the cultural forum of the World Wide Web than sit passively in front of such an ancient medium as the television.[38]

This is true of my nieces, who are at this writing age 14, 13, and 11. When they were younger, they spent much time in front of the television, so much so that their father set time limits on viewing activity. Now, they hardly watch television at all, and Dad is setting time limits on their Internet activity.

Even though McLuhan's tag line is archaic, its legacy persists. For followers of Christ, this dictum is an unfortunate digression. Thomas Boomershine points out that there is a transformation over the course of biblical history from the oral communication of the Word to the communication of the Word in printed form, on manuscripts.[39] And yet, God was and still is able to communicate with God's people, and God's people are still able to discern and follow. The book of Genesis begins by asserting that God spoke, and it happened. The book of Revelation concludes by asserting that it is written here, and so these written words must be true. Whether oral or written the Word is transmitted.

Think about the difficulty for Jews of Jesus' time. Many were resisting the onslaught of a Greco-Roman, manuscript culture and clinging to the sacred roots of their oral tradition. We grow to appreciate the apostle Paul, for Paul in following Christ is intentionally abandoning much of the theology but also the methodology of his religious and educational upbringing.

In terms of methodology, Paul describes his previous way of life: "I was advancing in Judaism beyond many Jews of my own age and was extremely zealous for the traditions of my fathers" (Gal. 1:14 NIV). Paul's rapid rise within the religious elite of early Judaism, and his presence at Stephen's stoning, demonstrated that he was not just set on preserving the sacredness of rabbinic Judaism but also the sacredness of the traditions and rituals for encountering God. He was likely to become one of the leading authorities among Pharisaic Judaism, which gave us the Mishnah and Talmud. But Paul's dramatic conversion completely altered his vocational path. It took him away from the oral, rabbinic traditions of the Temple religion and to an entirely new methodology that utilized the highest technology of the time: manuscript writing delivered via the Roman infrastructure and away from the Temple. As he later wrote in his letter to the church at Rome, his encounter with the risen Lord contradicted a lifelong belief that his ability to encounter God is a by-product of his ability to uphold the letter of the Law.

The magnitude of Paul's conversion mirrors the shift that the twenty-first-century church must make from modern to digital culture. In telling Paul's story in the book of Acts, the author Luke is pointedly saying to the Jews of his day that following Jesus means (among other things) a shift out of the Temple and its oral tradition and into the agora (marketplace) of Greco-Roman, manuscript culture. With a wide glance at these cultural shifts in communication, we see that the Word is communicated in oral and written forms, and this encourages us that the Word can also be communicated in the multisensory media of the digital culture. If this seems a frightening leap, remember that the medium is *not* the message. Rather than worry about the proper reverence for God's Word—to which the present authors bear faithful witness—be more concerned that methodology (orthopraxis) is usually more difficult to change than sectarian theology (orthodoxy), which the present-day change agents acknowledge from studying the book of Acts.

The shift we are facing today is reminiscent of Paul's story. The church is loaded with scribes, professors, and religious elite whose career investment is in the modern, print culture. Making the shift to digital culture is an insecure risk, and yet a few are following the call of Christ.

Digital storytelling as an act of grace

After we finished speaking at a pastors' retreat on the use of screens in worship, a pastor rose and began to explain his thinking about the placement of screens in his sanctuary. He indicated that his church made the conscious decision to put screens on either side of the sanctuary, rather than the middle. This allowed the symbolic focus to remain where it should, on the representations of the cross and the altar. Media, he said, should be servant to the Word.

This type of conversation is part of the reluctance in thousands of congregations that are deciding whether to embrace digital culture.

There is often an inability to differentiate between the Word and the mediums in which the Word is communicated. This gap is indicative of a much deeper theological problem for the Church. Some of God's leaders say that, much like the ancient Israelites, there are conditions appropriate for appearing in God's presence. God's presence may come and go, and we as followers of God may do or build certain things that summon or turn away God. This theology of presence draws from the priestly Old Testament tradition that God's presence is fixed, such that God lives in the Holy of Holies within the Temple. With this theology of presence, some leaders turn to the Old Testament to find communication symbols, such as sacrificial altars to stimulate the summoning of God's presence.

J: Because we are now twenty centuries away from encountering or summoning God via animal sacrifices, we Christians have gradually learned that sacred environments are for our awareness of the continuous, present reality of the Holy Spirit—not to summon God. The God of the New

Testament is already present, before, during, and after worship. Jesus taught us to be careful about worshiping the symbols of the faith. So did the prophets in the Old Testament, because symbols are not the object of worship. If they are, they become idols. There is nothing innately holy about a block of wood, a chunk of glass, or a piece of cloth. The screen is no less or more holy than the altar that might be located below it.

These idolatries make it difficult for churches that want to incorporate digital media into their worship. Some say they cannot shift into more relevant media because there is no place to put the screen: "The cross is in the middle of the sanctuary, and the pipe organs are on the side, so there's nothing we can do."

L: Jesus radically taught and demonstrated that through him God abides in us, and that our worthiness is not a condition of our holiness. In spite of his ability to communicate within the oral tradition of the Sanhedrin, even at an early age, Jesus chose to communicate by using different methodologies. He constructed his message into parables, using symbolic language that is not linguistically above the understanding of the general public, which in the present day we would call a sixth-grade reading level. Jesus also spoke to the ostracized persons of his day. The ostracized persons of our day are those who are not educated or who choose not to participate in the high-culture traditions of the Enlightenment. Jesus mandated through his teaching and healing that we reach this very audience, the "hungry or thirsty or a stranger or needing clothes or sick or in prison" (Matt. 25:44 NIV).

In Jesus we are not dependent on the forms and practices of the priestly Law. In the Holy Spirit we have with us the summation of the Law, the resurrected Christ. Jesus satisfied for once and for all the requirement of the Law and in so doing reconciled us to God, making us worthy and able to experience the presence of God through the abiding presence of the Holy Spirit. This radical concept of God abiding in us, of grace, got Jesus killed by religious leaders who were intent on maintaining their established religious systems of how to communicate with God.

This stubborn Temple theology that Paul rejected in his conversion drives faulted thinking in our churches today that there are levels of sacredness and levels of profaneness. How could the holy exist in such dirty places as we find in our culture? How could we find the sacred in the same places where we find pornography and violence? The rejection of digital media and digital culture, or even the idea of using digital media only as a priest engaging culture in a missional sense, or for the sake of bringing people into the faith, assumes that digital forms should be subservient to more holy forms. In a previous work I labeled this: "Media as Evangelism."[40]

But in Christ, whether those places are dirty urban streets or television sets, there may be God, a light in the darkness. The Incarnation is defined as God choosing to get dirty, illuminating the dark places, and redeeming television's messages. This is the true model of Jesus' communication style. Not that we must use the "more profane forms," and get our hands "dirty" in order to point people to the holy places where God really is, but that we see all forms as capable of transmitting the Good News of the grace of God through Christ Jesus. To truly be a disciple of Christ we must not stay in the comfort of the "sacred" places and the rituals of our comfortable religious milieus, but rather we break down the barriers that separate Jesus from those who have not yet had the joy of celebrating Christ.

Robert Webber has helped many churches make the blended leap from a formal literate practice of worship to an informal literate practice. This view has helped many church leaders, but those churches are likely to hit a wall when advised that worship arts are servants (or supporting actors) to the "text of worship." He states that "technology" (by which he refers as a broader definition to digital culture) is best deployed for evangelism and not for the people experiencing God in worship.[41] Such a position could hold that arts are central to the worship experience, as many church leaders now admit, yet still not understand the relationship of technology and art, and by extension technology and an experience of God. This is a particularly difficult leap for moderns, who are trained in the ubiquity of book technology and rooted in its forte of textual analysis. Every communication medium is able to reflect the glory of God. The value of digital art is not merely found in how well the congregation understands the "text" of a particular worship experience. While these themes are certainly important, there is another level of art as experience, or presence, in worship.

A pastor of a church in Queens (New York) tells us about his problem of creating meaningful worship for four different worship services, to four different language groups, each averaging 100–150 persons on a weekend. Orally translating every spoken word was utterly cumbersome and destroying the energy of the Word. So they have turned to visual art, using resources to create "wordless worship," or worship without having to translate everything orally. They decided to communicate the Word by displaying graphic images and photos that transcend cultural and language barriers. Pastor Ron Tompkins says that through art they have finally found the means to unite each of their various cultural communities. Visit this dynamic church at www.onechurchnyc.com. Art is not servant to the text of worship, or to the ideas in the text. Visual art, spoken word, music, and any other medium are potentially adept, with surprising pathos, at transmitting the Gospel.

Worn-out words: forming new models for digital age worship

Nobody knows what label to use for digital media in worship. We use adjectives, such as

- Contemporary (a loaded word that could mean heavy metal just as easily as it might mean "Pass It On" around the campfire)
- Multisensory (yes, we engage the senses, but the senses do not validate true worship)
- Multimedia (yes, we use moving and still images, but this convergence of media in worship is too often misunderstood as dispensable embellishments or objects, as if ornaments are hanging on a tree)
- Wired (yes, we use technology, but we don't say organ worship, which also uses technology)

- Worship and the Arts (yes, art is crucial, but the moderns coined the term to mean *fine art,* which is not what defines worship in the digital culture.)

The mushrooming list of adjectives to describe worship for digital culture is frustrating. Each has its advantage but fails to sum up the experience of worship in the presence of God. Perhaps this is because semantics are an exercise inherent to modernism.

J: The word *contemporary* is of course a product of whatever culture its users find most relatable. Some planners create worship that is contemporary to them, whether that be contemporary 1950s with the pipe organ and four-part harmony, contemporary 1960s and 1970s with acoustic guitars and folk music, contemporary 1980s with electric guitars, keyboards, drums, and endless praise choruses, contemporary 1990s with hip-hop, rap, and "boy bands." Each form (dominated by musical relevance) becomes sacred, or made holy.[42] Because God's presence was so apparent at one time in these forms, it is turned into a formula for how to worship in the particular decade, if not the distinct generation.

L: Jesus' preaching style is potentially helpful in defining "digital age worship." In Mark 4:33-34, Jesus is observed proclaiming the Word exclusively through many parables. Parables are the primary way in which people understood what he was saying to them. "He did not say anything to them without using a parable." Jesus didn't simply use parables as an alternative for the stupid ones in the crowd. Parabolic teaching through simple, fictional stories is his only public method for communication.

One reason may be the larger the crowd, the shorter the attention span. In large crowds, people don't have the opportunity for the dialogue and feedback that come from effective analysis. The parable is best suited for one way, large group communication. The teaching that comes from tackling deeper issues is best left to a small group environment in which people are free to discuss, compare, and discern the truth.

J: By now some readers may be worried that digital worship methods—particularly with respect to scriptural authority and sacred symbols, described in this book—are too radical. We take a cue, however, from Jesus, who was skilled at creating artistic stories to which people could relate. For example, who was the prodigal son? Was he from a family that Jesus knew personally? Perhaps, but it is just as likely and wonderful that Jesus used his imagination to tell a story about a "make-believe" character, to communicate some very important lessons about grace. The contemporary analogies, metaphors, and stories aided listeners in their understanding of his teachings. His use of artistic characters and plots raised questions that he could then answer later in a small group setting.

L: The public presentation of the Word is offered in the form of morsels, through extended metaphors, to inspire the receiver to ponder life in Christ. This is our example. The purpose of digital media is not to add further complexity to an already difficult presentation of abstract ideas like "grace." Media isn't even best deployed to echo oral presentation through points and scriptures on the screen, no matter how colorful. Digital narrative is an ideal medium for the parabolic function of the present day, to help the community of worshipers become aware of the presence of God in their midst. Jesus used the story form of parables through oral telling; we can use the story form of parables through digital experience. Jesus spoke in parables "as much as they could understand," or "as they were able to hear." In other words, they were getting the message! Digital media is the best way for us to complete Jesus' metaphorical statements that "the kingdom of God is like. . . ."

Contemporary? Traditional?— Authentic

Regardless of whether they are operating within traditional, contemporary, or some other worship format, the biggest problem most churches face is dealing with the upcoming Sunday. How does digital age worship fit into the current mix of traditional and contemporary worship services found in your church?

Tens of thousands of churches are either now wholly "contemporary" or have started contemporary worship services to offset their "traditional" worship services. Both styles of worship are market driven, in that they cater to the needs of their target audience. Churches sometimes label these audiences as "believer" and "seeker," and will often categorize the traditional service as believer-oriented and the contemporary service as seeker-oriented. Others combine these target audiences in "blended" worship, where both styles are often diluted to the point of being ineffective. The distinctions are frequently political, not theological, and manifest themselves in the wide variety of musical styles. Within the two prominent worship styles of "contemporary" and "traditional" is a wide variety of nuances. The differences between the two types are often related to form. Among the traditional style, we're all familiar with the country church that attempts to do high liturgy, but with little form.[43] This is the "old-time religion" church: "okay, now let's have a prayer." More common are the tall-steeple liturgical churches, which are often downtown, which broadcast worship, which is almost as compelling as watching paint dry.

On the other hand, worship is more often low in both liturgy and form among contemporary churches. Many of these services emphasize authenticity over excellence as a response to poorly executed worship that follows a detailed liturgical form during the Christian year. They advertise themselves to their community as over against the establishment: "Bored by church? Come to our church!" with an accompanying photo of people sleeping in their pews. Because of its associations, then, the use of digital technology in worship is mostly associated with a loss of form and presentation, which has a tendency to create a showy, shallow service.

In both styles, people are dissatisfied with the modern trappings of faith and its focus on objective empirical knowledge. Modernity has killed wonder and mystery. There's a vacuum that liturgy used to fill in the culture of Christian history that's been stripped away. People in our culture are looking for ways to replace it.

Some advocates within Anglo-Catholic traditions suggest that to revitalize Christian worship we should sustain modern-era liturgy but with more excellence. Consider the views expressed in a conversation I had with a woman in her thirties (to show that disagreement is not strictly generational):

1. Contemporary worship manipulates people's emotions. It is "cynical or callous or manipulative" to put together a church service and think specifically about how to create "heart moments." Or, to purposefully put things into the service to evoke emotions to make people want to come back and to increase the "stickiness" of the church. To be aware that those things are being intentionally created makes me not want to respond to that, even if I feel something.
2. It is bothersome to see "acting" in church. Music doesn't bother, movie clips and then discussions about the movie don't bother, but seeing someone's "performance" and then celebrating it as if we were at the theater is bothersome.
3. Communicating via different mediums feels like "entertainment." It feels like the church is trying to entertain people to get them to come back. As a contrast, formal liturgical churches have specific predictable liturgical functions in the service that "seem more aligned to the goals of what the church is motivated to do."
4. It doesn't feel natural to sing some of the songs, or to join in with everyone else who seems wholeheartedly sold on what is being "communicated" each week. It becomes "trying to fit into the group," rather than worship, to sing along. It feels like watching someone else's worship.
5. Finally, there's rarely any "quiet time" or "dead space" in the Sunday morning service. If the prayers are being led, there's no time to have individual prayers and thoughts and have reactions to that. And there's not any time set forth on Sunday to allow that to happen.

One of the problems with early digital age worship planning is the confusion of pace and noise, or activity. Pace is extremely important. But this is not the same thing as noise. Digital age worship planners need not be afraid of silence. It is a crude analogy, but the filmmaker Cameron Crowe used silence and pause to accentuate, not diminish, the experience of the relationship of Jerry Maguire and his girlfriend in his film of the same name just before they kiss for the first time. The pause is high contrast to the pace of their interaction and the style of the film up to that point. Pause becomes meaningful, and not boring, in the context of a well-paced experience.

J: During one worship event, the speaker began a retelling of Paul's conversion experience. The manner in which he told it immediately caught my attention. The house lights went down. Music and sound effects were perfectly timed with his words. Lighting changes enhanced the various moods throughout the story. Paul's story came to life right before my eyes. This story was produced with extreme excellence. I was deeply moved. And then with no transition and no time for reflection, the pastor instantly jumped back into his message. I was abruptly jerked from the moment and was lost to his words for the next four or five minutes. As with turning the lights on in a dark room, you must give the heart and soul a chance to adjust.

L: As we move further into digital culture and become more mature in our practices, we as the church will realize that worship remains the same. People still seek an encounter of God through such "traditional" elements as Scripture, Communion, prayer, community, contemplation, participation, and an awareness of transcendence.

Worship is more than the artifice of an emotional high. The goal of worship, whether oral or digital culture, is to tell the story of the risen Lord, and through it to glorify God through proclamation, prayer, and presence, and because of it to edify each other as the community of Christ. Digital age worship of the sort we advocate connects people to what God has done and continues to do for us, so that we may fully understand and experience the love of God. This subsequently leads us to a fuller understanding of what a relationship with God is about.

Continuity and discontinuity can be deployed intentionally to help people become aware of God's presence. I visited a church shortly before Easter. They had a powerful "contemporary" musical arrangement of the hymn "When I

Survey the Wondrous Cross," performed by a rock band, which was followed up by a sermon from a topical series on marriage that was still hanging around from Valentine's Day. The disconnection I experienced from the song to the sermon was disappointing. We see churches who put a lot of effort into creating powerful individual worship components for digital culture, many of which are excellent examples of the experiential components of sense, feel, think, act, and relate, only to diminish the experience by not having a broader sense of presentation or liturgical function, which of course traditional churches have a better chance of having because they are working with the polished modern-era liturgy. Being "sophisticated" or "slick" about digital technology is actually learning how to integrate the technology into high form, so it is not so deconstructed, and so the content of the experience can transcend the form.

For many people who are tied to a Christian heritage that is heavy in Christian-year liturgy, connection to God and to the presence of God is defined in terms of mystery. This is particularly true for Catholic, Orthodox, and some Anglo-Catholic Protestant traditions. Ironically, even though most Protestant churches hang on to the same framework, they are extremely low on the mystery scale, which may be a result of hundreds of years of using worship to indoctrinate and perpetuate systems of belief that may be divisive in their minutiae.

In any age and liturgical style, people seek the sense of the presence of God that worthy worship provides. For our age, meaningful worship marries awe with digital technology. This holy awe does not have much to do with "traditional" versus "contemporary" worship forms. Digital age worship has the ability to re-introduce the mystery in worship that so many people fear has been lost. (When it comes to being disciples, swapping mystery for knowledge hasn't done wonders for most of us.) It throws away the false constructs of contemporary and traditional in favor of a singular experience that synthesizes the best of what has come before with the best of the present culture's media. In the digital age encountering the presence of God in worship happens not through analysis but through an experience that educates and transforms.

Digital age worship redeems cultural expression

On the web, I found an evangelistic rendition of the four spiritual laws. One church that posted it on their web site boasted, "Seven people a day are accepting Jesus!" Though the Holy Spirit can work through unexpected channels, I wondered if those seven people who clicked the "yes" button on that site each day had

any connection to worship, other believers, or a model of what Christian living should be, to sustain them past their initial moment.

In the tradition of Protestant evangelism, the camp meetings of the colonial days established a model of worship as the prime opportunity to evangelize, or "save souls." Although the context has faded from its early moments, the emphasis on "soul winning" is based on the idea that the world is evil, as well the culture in it. Since the world will end soon, so the thinking goes, we need to save as many souls as possible before it is too late. Without demeaning the importance of salvation, repentance, or the pervasiveness of evil, I think that this theology establishes a one-dimensional emphasis in worship that ignores the whole person and the culture in which we live. Such a focus actually hinders the advancement of the kingdom of God, because it creates an atmosphere of piety that sees walking the aisle in worship as a religious rite of passage, which is divorced from our continuing daily life in the culture at large. Proper evangelism is based in the whole person. The biblical mandate is to make disciples, not merely save souls.[44]

However, to do so, we must acknowledge that the culture is not 100 percent evil. John the Baptist calls us to purify our hearts in preparation for Jesus by separating the wheat from the chaff, or the pure from the evil, and throwing out the rest in the unquenchable fire (Luke 3). Similarly, each day, as media bombard us, we must do the same with the culture of our world, by finding the good and redeeming it for the sake of evangelizing whole persons, including their forms of expression.

In the last half of his letter to the Romans, after his long explanation of the grace of God, Paul says that the way to bring the whole person into the kingdom of heaven is by encouraging an authentic worship of God. As we strive to abide in the presence of God and to express that relationship corporately, it changes us, as Paul says, into a community that exhibits the fruits of the Spirit to one another and to the world. Of course, that impact is visible to those around us. Our changed lives have more to do with evangelism in a postmodern world than any strategy of soul winning could accomplish, because it is an authentic expression of what God is doing through the stories of individuals, not an empirical, doctrinal mandate of spiritual law.

This relationship between worship and culture is crucial. Worship must be rooted in its indigenous culture in order to be authentic both to worshipers and to outside observers. While studying Luke 3 as part of our work, we found an expression of John's truth through the contemporary example of the coffeehouse. In a coffeehouse, people are obsessed with brewing perfect pots of coffee that contain the pure flavor of the coffee bean. To get the flavor, it is necessary to extract it from the grounds of the bean, after which time the grounds are useless and are thrown away. We implemented this idea in a devotional moment at a conference, in which we had coffee brewing and cups available for drinking. We established the story motif with a graphic and a video, told the story from Luke 3, and had participants write on coffee filters the thing or things in their life that needed to be purified in order to be prepared for the coming Christ. Many participants indicated that the combination of elements regarding purity gave them a deeper sense of God's presence in purifying their hearts than anything they had ever heard preached from that scripture.

Instead of forcing people to abandon their world, which most do not inherently see to be evil, such reinterpretations of the Gospel allow people to experience a worship of God that is both indigenous to their culture and an authentic expression of God's presence.

J: And because they are present in the culture, the culture serves as a daily reminder of their worship. When people return home and hear a song on the radio that was sung in worship, when they see a film again that was used in worship, and even when they return to the coffee machine on Monday morning, the Gospel is working and shaping the heart.

The aspects from digital culture we use in worship sometimes cause worshipers to reconceptualize the world around them. One woman told me that I "ruined" (in a positive way) her cinematic experiences because she was continually reminded of a particular message we presented by using movie trailers as a metaphor.

L: For many persons the connection of God's presence and their culture has never occurred. When people find meaning and value in their forms of expression and behavior, it allows them to acknowledge that God wants their whole person, and not "just" their soul. It demonstrates to them that they don't have to abandon the culture of their heritage and daily life, but that God will meet them where they are and guide them through a transforming experience in which they truly may discover what it means to be completely, fully human. And the avenue for a greater awareness of our humanity, loved by God, is digital art.

So far in this project, we've analyzed the primary digital media model of the church, the "multimedia" approach, and how fundamentally different it is from the very digital culture it is being used to reach. We looked at a new way of approaching worship that both values and incorporates art as a key form of expression for digital culture. And we have discussed the necessity of discarding old cultural wineskins in order to discover art that is native to the rapidly growing tribe of digital culture.

If our culture is now truly built from digital DNA (anyone that is plugged in will have a hard time arguing this), and digital is the language of this collective tribe of which we are a part, then to do anything less than create worship that is

true to the digital DNA is racist. Chapters 6–9 will explain
how to use digital art to tell stories of Jesus that can "hot
sync"[45] with the digital tribe.

38. Tapscott, pp. 25ff.
39. "The Polish Cavalry and Christianity in Electronic Culture," Thomas
Boomershine, *United Seminary Journal of Theology* (1996), p. 4.
40. Wilson, *The Wired Church*, p. 24.
41. Robert E. Webber, *Ancient-Future Faith: Rethinking Evangelicalism for a
Postmodern World* (Grand Rapids, MI: Baker Books, 1999), p. 113.
42. *Worship Leader* (July/August) 2001.
43. Tex Sample refers to this as "soul" music in his book, *The Spectacle of
Worship in a Wired World* (Nashville: Abingdon, 1998).
44. J: Francis Schaeffer addresses this problem for the evangelical church:
"Many artists and thinkers have been honest in dealing with the consequences of their world view and have had the admirable courage to carry
it to its logical conclusion—which is much more than has been done by
many Bible-believing Christians who superficially accept Christ as Savior
and go no further. I don't mean that they are not saved, but their attitude
is 'Now everything's fine and we're going to heaven; that's the end of it.'
They go to church and sing songs to make themselves feel good. But if
Christians would push on in their faith, they would be out on the streets."
45. The term used to describe the synchronization of a PDA with a desktop computer.

Chapter 6
Making Digital Age Music

J: In high school I played bass guitar in the jazz band. Sometimes the complicated riffs would throw me, and I'd get lost in the music. It wasn't more than a few seconds after losing my place that the band director would tell us all to stop. He'd look me in the eye and say, "You dropped out! When the bottom goes, the music dies."

It wasn't that I was more important than anyone else; it was that each member of the band had an equally important job to do. We were all playing equally important instruments that when brought together made beautiful music. **(Experience "Tune It Up," Chapter 24 on the DVD.)**

In our view, digital media functions much like one of the instruments in the band. Each of the components of worship has a different part to play to make the melodies and harmonies work. So for instance, if you leave out the prayer in worship, one of the instruments is missing, and the music dies. Leave out the sermon, or digital media, and the same thing happens.

Unfortunately, some churches write their "jazz piece" without incorporating media and they then try to tack it on at the end. Have you ever heard someone try to play a lead solo over music that wasn't written with a solo in mind? It sounds like a muddy mess. When composers write music, they must specifically compose breaks for lead solos, so when a sax or guitar takes off it sounds like it fits. When we plan all other aspects of worship we must incorporate media from the beginning. It has to be written into the jazz of worship. Throwing sermon points or a video clip at a media minister on Sunday morning is a muddy mess.

We should strive as digital age worship planners to give equal attention to all the instruments of worship. The results of these efforts will make music that plays in perfect sync with melodies and harmonies that will touch the hearts of all who hear it.

Some people are of the opinion that the media should "serve" the other more established portions of worship. I would have been insulted if someone told me that my bass playing was only there to serve the drums or the brass section, and so on. All elements of valid or authentic worship should be celebrated. They are there to "serve" the Gospel rather than one of the other instruments.

An improved interface for worship

L: Frequently we hear that "contemporary worship" is such a production! There are multiple reasons that lead people to make such an assertion, including confusion between faith and culture. The primary reason for the complaint is that people have somehow become aware of the production aspect, or interface of worship, and the work is interfering with their ability to experience God.

An interface is, among other things, as "a common boundary shared by two devices, or by a person and a device, across which data or information flows, for example, the screen of a computer . . . or the set of commands, messages, images, and other elements allowing communication between computer and operator."[46] It is also "the place, situation, or way in which two things or people act together or affect each other or the point of connection between things." An interface is a point of intersection between people and also a dynamic action that has an impact on the people to which it connects.

Good interfaces are important because they make communication possible without getting in the way. Take e-mail, for instance. AOL continues to be successful as an interface because it markets the dream of transparency—even though the reality is much different. People don't really want to log on, configure dial-up addresses, wait four to five minutes, or even boot up the system and then open up an application to get their e-mail. They should be able to walk up to a cold computer, hit a switch, and receive their e-mail. The same for cell phones. Having email capability combined with the portability of a cell phone is nice, but not if it requires that I spend thirty minutes hitting each number key three or four times to get the letter I want. The interface for e-mail should be as transparent as ripping open a glued piece of paper. Whether it is e-mail, interpersonal communication, or worship, good interfaces don't get in the way; they facilitate.

This is because good interfaces are oriented to the user, not the system. Early research of personal computers focused on two different agendas.[47] One was a file-sharing idea that focused on the linear interaction of information; the other was a sensory rich, high-intensity graphic-user interface (GUI) and application. Each camp believed it was creating a superior interface that created the least amount of interference: the command line because it taxed the hardware less, and the GUI because it seemed more natural from a user's perspective. These revealed themselves in the marketplace as DOS versus the Macintosh (or Windows), or the command line interface versus the GUI. DOS won for many years, but eventually the graphic interface took over, as hardware capability caught up to the vision, because it was more human-like. It focused on the perspective of the user rather than the structural needs of the computer hardware. (DOS has become a metaphor for modernism, and GUI for postmodernism.)

A better interface for the world of computers doesn't mean better buttons, or sleeker, more industrial design, like putting beige hard-drive boxes inside iridescent blue boxes because Apple Computer did it. The long-term vision for the computer industry is to eliminate buttons, keyboards, and mice altogether, and to create an interface that is essentially organic.[48] People should be able to talk to their computers instead of getting carpal tunnel syndrome from typing so much, and they should be able to access the Internet anywhere, without having to use cumbersome machines, and they should be able to navigate a personal planner without learning alternate languages like "Graffiti."

As we see all of these dreams for digital communications, we find parallels to the Church's position. As with the aim of technological industry, worship needs to improve its sensory points of contact. It's similar to the creation of what the computer industry calls "personhood," or the design of intelligence. Worship for any age needs to acknowledge human need and respond to it with the Gospel.

The current apparatus of "contemporary worship" is clunky right now because it is only partially fitted to the needs of digital culture: "Transmitting freely from one to another is really where the field of multimedia is headed."[49] Oh, that the Church could transmit freely from one environment to another! As digital age worship matures, it will take on forms that are more rich and organic, and more reflective of its age, just as four-part harmony on the organ so clearly reflected the cultural sensitivities of the Enlightenment. Worship needs an improved interface for the whole of digital culture.

This means rethinking the entire interface of worship, not simply making "better buttons" in the way of better bulletins or putting lyrics on the screen instead of in hymnals. We need to facilitate worshipful encounters with God that transcend the interface on which they happen. We need to make the appearance of production, or the mechanics of worship, go away. Removing the mechanics, and allowing for a more organic experience, allows for a rediscovery of mystery.

J: Implementing digital age worship means raising the bar on production values associated with the worship experience. The culture of today is completely immersed in a world of incredible sights, sounds, and smells. When we ask for a show of hands for how many love to go home to watch public access television, the final tally is always zero. When the excellence factor is extremely low, people don't tune in. Instead CNN, ESPN, Lifetime, and many other high-end networks fill their screens. Whether it is worship or TV, people aren't engaged when the production is bad.

Maybe our approach in this age should reflect that of the local mall or coffee shop. Michael Slaughter describes how the coffee shop is a great model for the church in the digital culture. Where else can you set down in a comfortable chair, read a good book, smell fresh brewed coffee, while listening to a live jazz band in the background. Compare that to the local library, where (rooted in the modern era) food and drinks are not allowed, music is disruptive, and the chairs are often hard and uncomfortable. The coffee shop model invites us to an experience that is full of inviting sights, sounds, and comfort.

But some suggest that worship should not be a production. They fear that the "slickness" of the experience may take something away from the Spirit's movement. I must admit that I felt the same way when I first visited the early digital age worship experiment at Ginghamsburg Church a year before joining the staff. I thought church should be what I had grown up with, which was something much more formal. At the same time I was serving in YoungLife, which strived to bring the gospel to the youth in ways that were relevant to them. I began to see that using digital media made the Gospel come to life in ways that were real for people of this culture including me. Without the production this could not happen.

The production nature of worship isn't new. Worship has always been a production! In *Out On the Edge*, Mike Slaughter says:

> The pre-literate church made rich use of imagery. The medieval churches in Europe depended on the visual arts to tell the biblical story. Elaborate wood and stone carvings, massive stained glass windows, tapestries, frescos, and detailed paintings by the masters mixed with dramas that were often used as interludes in the sermons. This appeal to the senses made the Church the best multi-media experience in town. Candles and incense added to the multi-sensory environment. The ritual, with "bells and smells," was intentionally designed as pictures for the senses. (p. 75)
>
> "The visual arts were so central to the presentation of the gospel in the middle ages that they even influenced the ways preachers spoke and gestured! Late medieval preachers were skilled performers who used a repertoire of gestures known to their audiences from paintings. Manuals of such gestures existed providing a stylized body language that accompanied and heightened the verbal communication." (Thomas Troeger, *Ten Strategies for Preaching in a MultiMedia Culture*, p. 12, as quoted in *Out on the Edge*.)

The craftsmanship and storytelling abilities required to experience worship that would speak to the culture of the day could easily be defined as production skills. The better honed they were the more effective the sermon or worship experience would be.

When we talk about producing worship we get an inevitable set of practical constraints. How do you keep up, how do you avoid burn out, (and my favorite) how can the Spirit do its work if everything is planned out? (We'll answer the first two in the next chapter.) The power of the Spirit cannot be limited by our efforts. No amount of preplanning can restrict the Spirit's presence in worship. As I mentioned earlier, I always feel closest to the Spirit when creating art for worship. Can we not trust the Spirit's presence in the formation and creation of the worship experience? Will it not then be present as the service is taking place? No matter how planned or produced worship might be, there are always unknowns. We should rely on the Spirit's guidance in all that we do, and especially in implementation of the weekly spiritual meal. As a production team we would always begin our worship experiences by praying for the Spirit's guidance. I can remember times when something unexpected would happen, like the pastor leaving the stage sick or drama lines being missed and so on. The team would begin praying on the spot that God would continue to guide us through whatever hurdle we were facing. Many times there was an almost tangible sense that the Spirit was hovering, assisting our every mood.

Some will ask the question: How do you avoid emotionalism when you begin to use digital media to communicate the Gospel? My first response is that what we do must be rooted heavily in prayer and Scripture. If we start and remain rooted there we avoid many potential problems down the road. Giving people an emotional or experiential connection with biblical texts is an important part of digital age worship. There is a big difference between manipulating worshipers' emotions and giving them an experience. We've already learned that digital DNAers crave experience, and so we must strive to be authentic in the way we present the stories of the Bible. Anything less may become empty and manipulative presentation.

Len often points out that the metaphors we use (and all art for that matter) are merely doorways by which to enter into an emotional understanding of biblical truth. Digital DNAers often cannot enter the room of biblical truth without an appealing doorway. The emotional connection with their own personal human needs is the key to drawing them into the room. Again, this is not emotionalism.

When we talk about GUI we're not just talking about the screen as the interface. The entire worship environment is accessible through the interface. There are many aspects within the physical worship space to consider, including lighting, sound, smell, taste, touch, video, alter display, animation, drama, dance.

During a conference in Orlando we took a day to visit a few of the local theme parks. After scouting the map we headed over to a ride called Poseidon's Fury, in Universal's Island of Adventure. The building was amazing. A large statue (three or four stories tall) of a Greek god looked as if it had been broken on the ground in front of the entrance. The entrance looked like a cave that was formed millions of years ago. Once inside we faced pyramid-like walls and candle lit halls. I remember both of us being totally astonished at how cool it was just to stand in line. Then we entered into a room with a circular stage standing about two feet off the ground. The room went dark except for a single spotlight, which shined on a ladder coming from a hole in the ceiling. From a ladder came an old man with a full beard wearing ancient clothing and carrying a cane. He made his way to the stage where he began to tell the story of Poseidon's battle with Zeus. Laser lights painted ancient figures on the walls. We were taken further into the story by entering various rooms, and ultimately ended up in a large room with images projected on screens and onto waterfalls. The storyteller interacted with the characters presented on the screens, as explosions of light, fire, and water went off around us. We were completely surrounded by the story, and it was fascinating.

If such amazing detail can be given to ancient myths, how much more to the truth of the Gospel! The same attention to environment is possible in worship. Worship leaders interacting with the screen, music overlapping dramatic storytelling, and natural elements such as candle flames and water can give worshipers the sense that they are part of the story. Unlike Poseidon's story, we have a different story, with a larger truth to share. As worship designers we should all have field trip money set aside to visit theme parks for creative inspiration. We can take advantage of the millions they spend on getting a theme or metaphor into production.

L: Redundancy is critical to the teaching aspect of worship. Good digital age worship has many different channels of communication, so that the worshiper has multiple opportunities to cull meaning from a number of different sensory devices. This is multi-modal—not time-sharing—or messaging back and forth, but more like face-to-face conversation, which has a constant dual interchange of meaning. In other words, digital age worship is not a modern presentation of a linear sequence of events, in which each event stops before another in singular fashion. Digital age worship is a multi-stack, or what Len Sweet calls a "double ring,"[50] a postmodern matrix of overlapping sensory experiences, or modes, that create a constant exchange of meaning. Digital age worship is GUI, not DOS.

Operating with assumptions

Creating a digital age worship interface means creating a matrix of media that operates within the interactive assumptions of digital culture. There are interactive assumptions with print or oral culture where worshipers don't acknowledge every typo in the bulletin or every grammatically misspoken word. In print and oral culture these assumptions don't interfere with communication. Worshipers move past an awareness of the form of communication, to an acceptance of its messages.

Nowhere is this more apparent than in the apparently anti-digital "Unplugged" movement of young people in the 1990s. The move to coffeehouses and acoustic guitars was not anti-technology but rather a preview of the future: post-technology, or the moving beyond (metastate) of self-awareness where we announce movie clips by saying, "Let's look at the screen." Digital media should take on this role in worship. The difference is not an abandonment of digital culture, but rather its integration into a more mature, organic system of interaction, or a more fully digital interface.

Ways to build a digital worship interface

1. *J:* **Overlap!** Transitioning from one portion of worship to the next can be critical to the effectiveness of the experience. Communication studies have shown that once you've lost the attention of your audience it can take twenty minutes to get it back. Thus if you lose them after praise and worship, and your thirty-minute sermon follows, you may only have their attention for the last ten minutes. Effective use of media can fill the potential holes in worship.

I liken digital age worship to the "pass the egg" game I played when I was in youth ministry. The game goes like this. There are two teams lined up next to each other with each team member holding a spoon. The egg has to be passed from one end of the line to the other without dropping it. First one to get the egg to the other end wins. This should be a delicate process, but in the spirit of the game the floor is covered with scrambled eggs. The worship moment is much like that egg for the individuals who fill our sanctuaries. When the stage is bare between elements, someone is fumbling with a microphone, or the sound system is turned off but the band is trying to play, the egg hits the floor. The screen not only makes the songs, sermon, and various other elements, more meaningful, it also covers those egg-drop experiences.

This does not mean that there are no pauses or quiet times in worship. In fact we advocate time to reflect on various pieces in worship. Using graphics and animation during some of the pauses in worship is a great way to use the screen. A main worship graphic can be the primary graphic displayed throughout a worship experience. Think of it as a default screen that can fill the visual "holes" in worship. There is no need for your screen to be blank at any time. The "default graphic" can provide smooth transitions between elements in worship. For example, when the call to worship has finished and the musicians are on their way to their instruments, put the graphic up to divert the attention of your congregation as this transition takes place.

2. Integrate the **metaphor** throughout. Making the move to metaphorical presentation of the Gospel means finding ways to make the metaphor work throughout the entire worship experience. Earlier we shared how metaphor is the glue to

make the Gospel message stick in the minds of worshipers. It is also the glue that makes the various elements of worship work as one. Metaphor cannot be effective if limited to the screen. This means that the worship leader's language; the pastor's message, the songs, and so on, must all together reflect the metaphor. It is worth saying again that the metaphor must be strictly rooted in Scripture.

Here are a few questions to ask that will help you integrate the theme and metaphor:
a. Do the songs reflect the theme/metaphor?
b. How can the altar space be used to further communicate the theme/metaphor?
c. Are there any smells associated with the theme/metaphor?
d. Are there any objects the worshiper can take with them to remember the experience?
e. Are there ways to alter sermon points, prayers, and other spoken words to make the metaphor work?
f. Can lighting be used to further integrate the theme/metaphor?
g. Can you sum up the experience in a few sentences?

3. *L:* Forge a new **synthesis** of all the best of Christian tradition. Digital age worship is not exclusively the latest and greatest but a combination of many forms, each that can express unique things. The phrase "Ancient-Future" is popular in progressive church circles because it connotes both innovation and tradition. Digital age worship doesn't deny tradition; it takes the best of it and rejuvenates it. One example is in biblical storytelling. Rather than just reading the scripture lesson, storytelling offers a way in which the hearer can enter into and internalize the story, as if they were present in first-century culture and hearing it for the first time. Although storytelling has found renewed enthusiasm in church circles for a few years, digital age worship takes the form one step further by introducing soundtracks, sound effects, lighting, fog, and imagery. The combination of these elements can create a much more powerful experience than in the traditional reading of the big dusty altar Bible, which I read publicly for worship as a teenager.

J: When you take each of these various traditions, cultures, and current forms and make them work together thematically, the result is something entirely new. When it works, it is a fusing together of elements that can make worship a powerful and timeless experience. If the hard work of tying it all together isn't done, the experience can become a muddy mess. This should be a primary concern when the worship planning team meets. Giving up early on making elements work thematically always results in an experience that is not at all memorable.

4. *L:* Be more **holistic**. Worship planners and leaders must become more holistic in their approach to both media in worship and worship itself, and begin to see media as both communication and communion. As the print age became more sophisticated, it distinguished roles such as reporter, layout designer, and press operator, or as power struggles dictated, the idea people and the production people. Recent technological changes have collapsed these boundaries and returned the communication industry toward an era of integration, much like the era when Shakespeare hung out in the pressroom.

Someone might say, "Well, what about the film industry, which is highly specialized?" The answer here is that the real trend in film isn't Hollywood and unions, whose structural system was built fifty years ago,[51] but in the democratization of digital production that is occurring everywhere through the iMac and the like, which is creating a whole new breed of independent filmmaker.

The holistic approach applies both to skill sets as individuals and to teams in service of the worship experience. We need not support superhero pastors who want to add digital to their skill repertoire, but rather empowering environments where consensus is the force that creates digital art for revealing God.

Artists of any age are holistic. They are good at the mechanics of form as well as expression. Michelangelo invented new techniques when working on the Sistine Chapel project because the project, in all its complexities, demanded a degree of craftsmanship that had previously not existed. Guy Kawaski, the Apple marketing guru, wrote Rules for Revolutionaries in which he uses the term "Evangineer" to describe a person who has a burning desire to change the world and the technical knowledge to accomplish it.[52]

It is a bad idea to separate the technical group from the creative group. Some members of the community seem more interested in widgets, and other members in ideas. Resist the temptation to allow these divisions to grow, for to truly be effective, a digital age minister must go through the painful work of learning both. I don't mean to the point of mastery, as each of us is gifted in unique ways. Teams that work are teams that understand enough about each other's gifts, skills, and interests to both communicate and empathize.

J: I'm not a preacher, but I've written and given what some would call sermons for various services over the last decade. Each time was a struggle, and I was often worried that what I would say might not relate, or would be confusing, or offensive, or ineffective. I hated that pressure. Then I joined a worship design team. Although my job on the team was not to preach, I felt a comfort in that what we designed in a group would work in worship because the material had been tested in our group. I don't ever want to go back!

I can't understand why anyone would want to work alone on worship when they could work with creative teams. When you work alone, a bad idea stays a bad idea.

A bad idea in a team environment is an opportunity for greatness. For instance, I might throw out a really bad idea for a metaphor after hearing the scripture for the week. Len might say, "Okay, that's a bit weird, but what about this . . ." You, in turn, might respond by saying, "I see where you're going with that, but what about . . ." and I might throw in one last spin on your idea to make it really work. Had I been working alone, the bad idea would have remained. When working in a team to design worship, ideas and creativity are exponential.

5. *L:* Pastors should broaden their self-conception from preacher to producer. Being a producer means one allows a team to co-construct the basic ideas of worship. This requires a great degree of control relinquishment. Give up some control. Don't worry about not getting credit or losing the most visible aspect of your job. Realize that good worship reflects good leadership. Broaden your self-definition to include not only

preaching skills but also leadership ability.

What about creating space for some bad stuff to happen? Yes, this could happen. But the essence of the team is in the core theology of the priesthood of all believers: each of us, through the work of the Holy Spirit, is able to encounter the Word of God. When people want to go crazy with their imaginations, allow them to be creative while holding them to core standards already present in the congregation, such as the mission of the church.

Sharing ownership of the worship planning function doesn't negate the preaching function or the role of teaching in worship. Both of these remain extremely vital in our digital world. Preaching is critical to discipleship, but the three-point sermon with illustrations may not be. Try approaching your sermons more like storytelling experiences. At the same time, take broader ownership of the entire worship service. Don't rely on the music person any more than the music person should rely on you. Work together.

J: Sooner or later many pastors become concerned that they will lose control. Although it shouldn't matter, credit becomes an issue. If a pastor works with a team, then it may seem as if their role is less than it once was. The pastor, however, might be perceived as the master planner who has reconceived worship for this age. All of the successes are attributed to the pastor. I look at it much like a baseball team. The pitcher is credited with the win, even though the whole team contributed in various ways.

6. *L:* **Don't compartmentalize**. It is not the job of the theologian to interpret and the technician to edit and the producer to form the story and then for them to all come together early Sunday morning to figure out how to link their work with some loosely held strand. For digital age worship, these functions should be mixed together in the formative stages of worship development. Being a digital storyteller is a holistic mix of interpretation and translation, integrity and integration, technical and creative. Not one person that does it all, but that they work together.

You may be surprised to find that creative empowerment will draw talented people to your ministry. So many gifted people don't put their gifts to ministry because the church insists that their music be acceptable to everyone in the congregation, that their stories and dance raise no questions, that their video challenge no prejudices, that their images maintain the status quo. God forbid that people should be challenged to move off their spiritual backsides!

7. Everyone on the team needs to **exegete culture** just as much as one might do with Scripture. To exegete means to reach in and extract the truth. Pastors are trained to do this with Scripture but not culture, though this flaw is slowly disappearing in many seminaries. We must learn how to extract truth from popular culture for the sake of completing the final step of the exegetical process, to put the truth of the Gospel back into the culture. Because we live in our current time and space, we must both pull out and push in truth with culture.

To truly exegete culture is a difficult, ongoing struggle. Culture is temporal and constantly changing. One cannot achieve a particular culture so much as one might achieve a particular moment in cultural history, which to be defined must be pointed toward a past cultural moment. This leaves the church in a position where it is never able to understand or relate to the culture of the present, which of course is what Jesus calls the church to do when it is commanded to promote the Kingdom of God. So we are called not to merely achieve or conquer a particular cultural language, but to stay in continual interaction with it for the purposes of communicating the language of the Gospel, which is both now and in the future, imminent and transcendent.

8. Allow the canvas for digital art to encompass the entire **worship space**, and not merely the drama stage or video screen.

J: When churches move in digital directions they often see the screen as the canvas. The screen is an important part of painting worship, but it should by no means be understood as the sum of digital age worship. There are so many ways to paint the picture, and sometimes the screen is not even needed to transform the moment. We often encourage churches to start without installing a screen at first. What does this look like?

Mike Slaughter was preaching on the seven disciplines from his book *Spiritual Entrepreneurs.* This particular week focused on the *biblical* principle. Our team wanted to present the Bible as an exciting record of God's love for humanity. The word *adventure* sprang up again and again in our design process. Someone suggested that *Indiana Jones and the Last Crusade*, a film popular at the time, might capture the adventurous spirit. The plot centers on the diary that Indiana's father kept throughout his lifelong search for the Holy Grail. Presenting the Bible as an adventure book, God's diary, would, we expected, help worshipers re-conceive the Bible in a fresh way. With the entire worship space as the can-

vas, we obtained the familiar Indiana Jones theme music by John Williams, and played it as worshipers entered the sanctuary. The house lights were low that week, with candles in lanterns, lighting each row of chairs. On the stage was an altar display that looked like a scaled-down version of what you'd find outside the Indiana Jones show at Disney's MGM Studios theme park. It was made of crates, rope, candlelight lanterns, the famous Fedora-style hat, and an old beat up Bible wrapped in a grocery bag. Mike even wore a kaki Indiana Jones shirt.

Worship began with a clip from the film. In it, Sean Connery explains the three challenges they must face to reach the grail. First, the breath of God, next, the word of God, and finally, the path of God. Those became the points for the sermon, so in a sense Sean Connery was our guest speaker that weekend. We altered the language for the prayer and all other connectional words throughout the service. Some worshipers were so drawn in by the experience that they returned for a second service.

Using smell and touch as part of the experience can also make worship more effective for this culture. We've had coffee brewing, Jambalaya cooking, incense burning, and we've even sprayed perfume on bulletins to engage the sense of smell. We've given out paper etch-a-sketches, shells, rocks, and pennies to give people a tactile experience of the word. The possibilities are broader than cinema when it comes to the canvas of worship.

L: Some tips:

a. Position your screen for maximum viewing. If possible, middle is best.

b. Use lighting to illuminate the speaker but not to blind or focus on the congregation.

c. Have stereo sound.

d. Create a flat, open public speaking space, perhaps even an "in the round" structure with a runway, similar to a fashion show runway.

e. Incorporate a combination of natural and artificial light, but don't let the natural light hit the stage or screen areas, only the worship seats.

Question:

If you can design your dream worship space, where money and time are no object, what would it look like? Brainstorm some ideas individually, or better yet, as a worship team. Now, after going through some options, how can you apply your dreams, and these ideas, to your current situation? Think of a couple of ideas that you can implement immediately.

f. Position the seats in such a way that will facilitate interaction. Don't make two rows of seats that all face forward! Create semicircles, or even circles.

g. Have space that can be altered to create various types of atmosphere depending on the needs of each worship experience. This could be like a film set or theater stage, but don't let it appear to be stark when unused, and not overly industrial or built primarily for elaborate, thematic production. The space needs to have the ability to be organic on its own, without an expensive set.

46. Microsoft Word Dictionary.

47. Negroponte, *Being Digital*, p. 95.

48. Ibid, p. 92.

49. Ibid, p. 71.

50. Leonard Sweet, *Soul Tsunami*, p. 27.

51. Thanks in part to efforts of Ronald Reagan.

52. Thanks to Steve Bentley for reference to Kawaski's book.

Chapter 7
Creating Digital Age Worship from Scratch

L: You are ready to become a digital storyteller, but perhaps lead less than a supersized congregation, with too little money and even less time. As you dream about the possibilities, there is undoubtedly a blue-haired demon on your shoulder saying, "You'll never get it approved!" You may feel like you are on a deserted island, where the only amenable character around is a volleyball.

How do you deal with a naysayer and get started? This chapter will outline a few approaches for how a small or medium-size church with little beyond traditional liturgy can create and implement strategies for creating digital age worship.

First, understand naysayers: They believe they're right. They are probably earnest in their complaints. So, first and foremost, demonstrate grace as you demonstrate passion. Love those who persecute you and your ideas. Realize that these naysayers feel that to leave the comfort of established traditions in worship and church life is the equivalent to leaving the rapidly shrinking oasis of truth in exchange for a desert of worldly practice.

J: Show them that you have an appreciation for their concerns. If they feel you're listening to them, you'll ease some of the inevitable tension in the air during the transition. They want to know that you understand the importance of the various church traditions that have been established long before you came along with projector in hand. Understanding those traditions can give insights into how to promote the new worship forms you're advocating.

L: The challenge of change-management leadership is how to plan and implement strategies that will navigate unwilling, ignorant, and fear-oriented people through a wilderness of change to a fresh and relevant place where worship both glorifies God and communicates to the people of digital culture.

Strategies for getting off the island

There are a number of strategies that change agents may adopt to get started with digital age worship.

#1 Demonstrate, don't debate

It is tempting as change agents to adopt a strategy where the majority of precious time and energy is spent trying to rectify incorrect theology, particularly for agents who have spent time studying the theology of the issue and have a slew of valid reasons why it is necessary to use media.

Getting caught up in theological debate reminds me of an incident that happened at home late one night at our apartment in Ohio a few years ago. I woke up to the sound of rushing water. Running downstairs, I discovered that a pipe in our rear storage room had frozen and exploded, spraying freezing water throughout the storage room. Water had begun to leak under the drywall into our kitchen. Although the only solution was to grit my teeth and shut off the water, it made more sense to my cold feet to lay down towels to stop the water that was rapidly covering our kitchen floor.

Trying to implement change through theological debate is analogous to stopping the flooding by absorbing the water. Although a proper understanding and presentation of the theological significance of media as a form for communicating God's truth is essential, polarizing debate won't change people's minds. I have discovered time and again that one finely produced, properly executed worship experience is more effective than a lifetime of roundtable discussions at demonstrating the power of the screen when communicating the heart of the Gospel.

J: Whether debuting a new building fund, starting a contemporary worship service, or making a media ministry, talk is cheap.

The same principles were true for me as I began to form a passion for animation in worship. I knew that the only way I would ever be able to implement its use on a regular basis would be to produce a few pieces in secret and present them completely finished. Most of the team didn't know I had been practicing on my off time, and they certainly didn't know that I was planning to walk into tech rehearsal that week with an animated call to worship. After popping in the tape for the first time for the team and seeing the team's reaction, I knew it would not be hard to convince them to do this again.

Prior to that demonstration, my supervisor walked by my desk while an animation program was open. He asked me what I was doing, and when I explained that I thought this might be something new we could try for worship, he told me to quit goofing around. I didn't give up. I just worked at night when no one was around.

L: Let's assume that you have experienced this catalytic experience in worship. There is a likelihood that, although many have "converted" to being media advocates, there are still those hardliners who refuse to give in, for a variety of reasons. Have you ever known people who, once proven that they are wrong, refuse to acquiesce? I have known people who would rather enter into a realm of complete irrationality than acknowledge another ideological possibility. Regardless of what you do, some people will never accept your leadership, whether it is in the realm of media, preaching, or what section of the parking lot to repave. *To steal a line from a friend,* "Put it up for a vote, and the people will always vote to go back to Egypt."

As a leader in Christ's church, it is your job to give compassion and love to these people while at the same time holding fast to the mission that you have been given. Although this may sound harsh, it is more important that these people stay within God's kingdom than your particular church. In Matthew 15, Jesus is confronted with a Gentile woman whose daughter was demon-possessed. Even as he healed her, Jesus was clear that his mission was to the lost sheep of Israel. He could not afford to spend his precious energy on Gentiles, who were to follow with the later mission of the church. Acknowledge that while each member of God's kingdom is precious, the time you have on this earth is as well. Stay positive to them, stay loving, but stay committed to your mission.

None of us want to see this sort of rift occur, however. Although it isn't foolproof, one way to avoid a rift is to enlist strategic lay leadership to assist with the vision casting. Key lay leaders can turn a programmed mandate into a grassroots movement. This difference in perception can go a long ways to overcoming negativity.

In addition to strategic lay leadership, it is vital to have two key staff people on board as well. The senior pastor and the music leader are the two most important contributors in the worship design process, and if either or both of these people aren't on board with digital age worship, it won't happen.

The problem is that for people in these positions who have been designing worship for often quite a long time, there is not a clear mandate to change. It is easy as a change agent to deride their efforts as out of touch or as an obstacle to creating a team-based worship experience. But you first need to respect that these people have been striving to create meaningful worship for a long time. That they continue to work as individuals reflects their training in models taught them by seminaries and mentors in ministry.

Your primary goal is to demonstrate a new model through the creation of a team environment for every aspect of worship planning, including music, calls to worship, and even the sermon. It is only through jointly prepared worship at every level that truly transforming integrated media worship may occur.

One of the tired formulas is the preaching model of three points with illustrations. This formula is likely to persist even after a pastor moves into projection during worship. Often, the pastor will call the media person into his or her office to preach the sermon on a Friday, or (worse) send the sermon by e-mail, and ask what graphics could be inserted. It is often demoralizing for the media person to be asked for "creativity" on demand. Bringing in two more people might improve the creative potential, but most still can't get past the model of appending visual ornaments to a completed talk. To overcome this AV mentality, try starting with the media and then building the sermon around it.

This tactic was a breakthrough for us at Ginghamsburg. Noted civil rights leader Otis Moss was in town for a theological seminary board meeting, and agreed to be interviewed for use in worship. Because of his schedule, we did the interview on a Wednesday. After the interview had taken place, I roughed together some video clips and the pastor viewed them on Thursday morning. Because the video of Otis Moss was so compelling, the pastor decided to write his sermon based on the clips. So for worship that weekend we used Dr. Moss and civil rights footage throughout worship and the sermon, and combined with other graphics, a drama and music, we created our first completely integrated worship experience. After that breakthrough we all had a deeper understanding of what it meant to be media integrated, not as an abstract idea or something related to one or two elements in worship, but something we had actually implemented.

Even a pastor with creative vision can get stuck in a situation with seemingly little money, creativity, or desire for change. In this situation getting the program staff and lay leadership on board means nurturing progressively minded people to assist in the worship process. Just as in the Dr. Moss example, finding specific weekends requiring their assistance and planning will demonstrate to them the nature of the model. This will raise the enthusiasm for a large number of your intended team.

After the shift is made, even more change is inevitable, or at least accelerated. For example, you might go through more transition in leadership than in modern era worship. Through every change in your worship planning team, continue to try out various members, changing the makeup of the team, until there is synergy.

#2 Don't spend too much money at first (Show the need)

It is not necessary to spend large sums of money to create a catalytic worship experience. The worship service featuring Otis Moss consisted of little else than talking head video and a few images of the civil rights era. The production values were definitely nothing to boast about. Yet the summary of the experience produced a synergy that went beyond its production values and the capabilities of our talent and equipment.

J: People often overlook simple ways that this can be done. Digital age worship is not necessarily dependent on a screen. You've already learned that elements such as metaphor, experience, participation, art, and music are essential for reaching digital culture. The good news is that employing most of these elements is completely free.

Almost every children's moment I have seen has focused on some sort of metaphorical object that generally relates well to the target audience of children. This is usually as simple as grabbing something off the shelf from home, or taking a trip to the nursery toy box. This applies even more to "adult" worship. The price tag for an object-lesson method is usually little or nothing.

Participation is also fairly inexpensive. You may be saying to yourself, "We already do that," but this goes beyond just allowing the congregation to yell out requests before prayer time. We regularly devise opportunities for participation in worship as part of the design process. During one service, we put together an Etch-a-Sketch weekend called "A Clean Slate." We made miniature versions of the popular children's toy with red construction paper and adhesive labels. Worshipers were instructed to write the things they wanted God to erase from their lives onto the (adhesive sticker) screen portion of their mini Etch-a-Sketch. They then had the opportunity to place those stickers on the cross. The fusion of music, prayer, tactile media, and physical movement toward the cross provided an emotionally powerful and memorable experience.

L: It is entirely possible to achieve significant results with only two televisions hooked up to a single VCR, showing clips from high-end feature films from Hollywood. Such little pieces of media will demonstrate the possibilities of the medium, and don't require much money. Church media pioneer Dennis Benson observed that money doesn't follow a budget line item; it follows vision. Whether it be organizations or families, if a project is embraced with enough passion, it is possible to find the money to make it happen. Passion is created through the excellent presentation of media's possibilities in worship (see above). A set of these experiences will begin to open doors for the money necessary to maintain a consistent presentation for the long haul.

#3 Start slowly

If a church has the people and equipment resources to put together a completely integrated weekend first time out of the gate, they are exceedingly rare. A more common scenario for a novice church, and one that is less prone to mistakes, is one in which a minor amount of media is used with excellence. This is more feasible both from a planning standpoint and an excellence standpoint.

One small church set up two TVs to a VCR and showed a clip from *The Christmas Carol* at Christmas. This was innocuous enough that the congregation didn't feel threatened, it was easy to pull off, and it fit well into the context of that pastor's sermon. A few examples of this can have the effect of creating enthusiasm not from the leadership but from the laity. Instead of being a forced mandate, then, changes in worship become mandates from the congregation.

J: Even in the most traditional of churches there are established times for doing things out of the ordinary. Children's moments, Sunday and Wednesday night services, Vacation Bible school, Easter and Christmas, are just a few of the times when an experiment is well tolerated.

One familiar example of permission-giving tolerance is when the pastor and music leader step aside to give the youth group an opportunity to lead worship. Take this opportunity to do drama, slideshows, and use music that is more upbeat and (in the opinion of youth) fun. The congregation is always happy to see young folks excited by their faith. They want to see youth more involved from time to time. Over a period of time the leadership may begin to incorporate some of the things that are attempted in youth-led services. Contemporary praise music becomes acceptable, and occasionally a drama. After a while begin to use PowerPoint to project lyrics in worship during the main traditional service. By starting slowly, and by demonstrating that the next generation wants to be at church, acceptance from the congregation may come with less pain.

L: Look for other places to try your ideas, such as in the education channels at the church. Worship may not be the best place to start, for the sake of both your congregation's acceptance level and your own expertise. You may have success in introducing film clips, original or purchased video productions, graphics and the like as a metaphors for small groups, Sunday school, or various other class environments. These locations, in particular, will allow you the chance to learn how to get in and out of clips, images, and music. These occasions allow you to practice integration.

Starting slowly, however, doesn't mean approaching implementation idly. Every week that passes into history is another week that the church is becoming further removed from the culture in which it resides. Slow integration is only apropos when it is strategic and not lazy. As the song by Petra states, "Good things come to those who wait/ not to those who hesitate."

#4 Don't mess up

J: They say that you never get a second chance to make a first impression, so you better not mess up! Avoiding mess-ups sounds a lot harder than it really is. Practice is a must. When you're set to begin planning for your first service be sure to give time for a dress or tech rehearsal. If you don't you'll regret it.

One pastor began a new job at a progressively minded church. They hired him partly because he had experience with using media in worship in his previous job. One afternoon he went in to convince his new team to use a film clip from the movie *City Slickers*. They hadn't done too much yet with film clips, but our friend assured them that it would be great. He told them that he had used this same clip before in a service, and that people responded to it. Sunday morning just before worship he handed the already cued tape to the media team. The time came to play the clip, and for the first time ever the staff and congregation watched in amazement. Then as the clip was finishing, Jack Palance dropped the big

"G**D***." Embarrassed, the pastor somehow preached a sermon. They didn't use a film clip for a while, and the next time they did, they cued it up, and practiced stopping it on time over and over before worship. Failure on our part to properly carry out what we've planned for worship only strengthens the naysayers' argument against what we're trying to do. So practice, and please get it right!

L: Even as a first-time experiment, there were problems with the use of the aforementioned *Christmas Carol* clip. The audio was not wired into the church's sound system. Instead, they turned up the audio coming from the little TV speakers, which came out distorted in their acoustically inferior worship space. This was especially troublesome since the clip they chose was from a black-and-white-era film that was difficult to both see and hear. Choose media that works within your space! And try it out ahead of time to see what the experience is like in the sanctuary, with respect to video and audio.

In addition, focus on doing well with limited things. This may mean simply using a film clip or one top 40 song, and working on completely integrating it, before you add a number of elements. Also, if, for example, your new service starts in September, use Sunday nights or other, smaller gatherings throughout the summer as an unofficial rehearsal environment. Find times to practice your new service before you go "live." Get together with your team(s) and plan exactly how you will get into and out of technologically intense moments. Plan at least three to four times where your team may actually go through the service in its entirety, without a congregation.

Excellence applies to production values and to lucidity of message. Speak something simply, so that everyone can understand, and use forms that are simply understood. Digital messages that come across muddled due to the lack of excellence are more detrimental than no digital messages at all.

#5 Use props; be creative

As you implement your plan within the congregation, focus on shifts in culture that pertain to the introduction of new technologies. Reread Chapter 2, Digital DNA. Think how you may introduce some aspect of digital culture into your sermon, the prayer, or some other aspect of worship.

Also consider how a focus on changes in culture may affect your service structure. For example, if you have already or are considering a "contemporary" service to off-set your "traditional" service, you may consider working toward integration of these two services. While it is true that "blended" worship, as it has come to be known, often does not work (because it is often a watered-down, mediocre version of both traditional and contemporary), the other danger is that you may end up with two antagonistic congregations. It may be possible to avoid this by demonstrating that technology and culture are two different things, and that what you are doing on Sunday evening is about culture, not technology. Cultural shifts may be subtler than huge screens hanging in the sanctuary.

This may mean that you don't use technology at all for a while. The point of media is to energize worship through making connections to the culture in which we live. Using black and white film clips and out-of-date music as elements, which may have a purpose in the proper context, can defeat the very purpose of media by being disconnected from our present culture.

Use props and objects in currently accepted moments in worship to open up the minds of your congregation to the use of metaphor in a worship environment. Incorporate them beyond a simple sermon illustration; for example, use the same prop to communicate similar themes in the call to worship, children's sermon, and sermon.

Creativity can be demonstrated in many ways, not all of which are directly related to screen use. One church in the Dallas area set up a chef in the sanctuary who cooked all morning while the pastor preached on the parable of the great banquet to which no one came. Both the visuals and the smells of the chef's presence made that morning a memorable one for that congregation. Further, screen use can tie together various creative elements. A simple banquet graphic would thematically reinforce the live chef element while providing ongoing visual art for the entire experience.

#6 Be consistent.

Another problem with the *Christmas Carol* example is that the church did little to follow up on the experience. An event like this requires strategic planning in order to lead to a more long-term holistic solution. For example, the pastor should include another film clip within a few weeks, followed by a clip somewhere else in worship within a month. A series of events over the course of time gives the model legitimacy through its varied use. Rather than debating the presence of the communication form as a discipline that needs to be addressed rather than assumed, demonstrate its nature through a consistent presentation. Properly executed, a pattern of use will reveal that digital media and screen use are not simply "toys," or "entertainment," but a viable form for the presentation of the Gospel.

J: Consistency in production excellence from week to week is important as you get going. After a while you'll want to set up a design standard. This doesn't mean that you have to make up strict rules for everything, it simply means that your design choices, colors, fonts, illustrations, and so on should feel like they're part of the same palette. Images shouldn't look the same from week to week, but should all be created with the same level of excellence and look as if they're from the same family. After a while your style will develop and evolve into something all its own.

When your team makes an effort to be consistent, it is inevitable that you'll want compare your current work with your previous work. This can be a dangerous trap. Learn from your past works, but don't let it haunt your present work. Having to live up to, or "one-up" yourself all the time is exhausting, and you can never keep up. Give yourself a break! Hundreds of movies are made every year but only a few are award winners. Not every week can have that award-winning feel. Sunday comes fifty-two times a year, and there will be a few duds. The Spirit will prevail when we don't.

#7 Bonus tip—Get the sound system happening

L: Your sound system is critical. Worship should be a sensory-rich experience, something that engages ear as well as eye. So put a major percentage of whatever money you have to spend into a sound system; for example, if given $50,000, you may invest $20,000 in video projection and/or cameras, $10,000 in computer and editing, and $20,000 for upgrades to your sound system. For more specific advice on how to invest in equipment, read Part 4 of *The Wired Church*.

While these tips provide the basis for a change strategy that can revitalize a congregation, there is always the distinct possibility that no amount of persuasive example may lead them away from their shrinking oasis. The decision whether to "shake off your feet," or leave them to their own devices, is one best left up to ongoing prayer and discernment with the Giver of your passions.

Creating a movie small group

One of the most appealing ways to nurture a spirit of digital age communication in your church is through the formation of a small group that watches and comments on movies. Watching movies with other Christians can be a fun exercise that helps your church get a better sense of the digital age. By watching movies, one can begin to engage in dialogue about their meaning, and it is through this that one can begin to understand more about how to communicate visually.

This dialogue can occur at three levels. One is through the story itself, or how the plot advances meaning. The second is through the underlying levels of the film, or the psychological, relational, and spiritual dimensions of the film. Like any good art form, more meaning can persist in a film than the artist/filmmaker ever intended. Good films often do this, particularly with respect to the spiritual dimension, whether because of or in spite of the intentions of Hollywood storytellers.

The third level of the film is in its form. Dialogue about this level will probe whether the framing, editing, color, filters, and so on, shape meaning in the film. A recent example of the use of color is the film *Traffic*, which intercuts three concurrent story lines. The rich traffickers in San Diego are shot in a soft yellow haze, the poor Mexicans in a gritty green, and the upper-class, urban legal people in Cincinnati in a blue. Each color makes a statement about the socio-political environment of its characters. A more classic example of color form is the use of red in *The Godfather*, representing of course blood and violence.

Talking about these sorts of things opens up a range of understanding about how to create your own digital art that communicates as effectively as good films do. For example, what sorts of colors are representative of Lent and Easter? Or of a weekend on anger and forgiveness? Most of the forms of film of course apply to video and still images as well. (In fact, the problem with much of video and the reason it is considered by many to be a stepchild to film is not its inherent technical structure but that its creators often have little to no understanding of these things.)

Encourage your movie small group to read about film. A good textbook for film that is fun to read with lots of illustrations is *Understanding Movies*, by Louis Giannetti. It is a college text, so it's expensive, but it is the indispensable book on understanding form. There are curricula series to help facilitate the discussion, such as *Reel Faith* for adults (Nashville: Abingdon Press), and *Reel to Reel* (Nashville: Abingdon Press), which is targeted to youth. Also, there are a number of current books on religious meaning in film. Each focuses on a few films and provides spiritual exercises related to the experience of viewing the film. Use these books sparingly; don't turn your small group into a college course. Make sure the group has fun together, but also have these books available as people begin to get more involved.

Question:

What unique start-up strategy could you use with effectiveness to start becoming digital storytellers?

Also, set some ground rules for your group, such as, do you watch the films together, or on your own? This largely depends on how much time you have available. If possible, a three-hour session with the film and then discussion afterward would be best, with e-mail follow-ups if people want to continue their dialogue. Also, what sort of movies do you want to watch? Of course, I'd recommend not just focusing on "bathrobe" dramas, or period pieces from the Bible, though these are certainly acceptable. Broaden your range to include good Hollywood films of some depth. You might consider focusing on directors, such as a series of Peter Weir films, or Stephen Spielberg, or Michael Mann, or upon whomever the group decides. Often directors have ongoing themes to their work, so doing them sequentially can be stimulating, by looking for similarities.

Other issues that might be appropriate include acceptable ratings, or whether the opinions of critics like Ebert are wanted. And make sure to watch them on DVD, and begin with the DVD's trailer, if it is on the disk. The trailer is a great way to set up the film experience.

Keep the momentum going

Increasingly, churches have already made some initial steps, including the presence of video projection in worship, and are now struggling with an entirely different set of challenges. These challenges revolve more around maintaining momentum. Worship is planned at least fifty-two times every year. Even network TV shows get summers off! Creating a transforming environment in worship means establishing a standard that survives and grows over time. Here's a list of ways that churches can maintain a high level of artistic quality over the long haul.

#1 Look for ways to be simple

I recently received an e-mail with a few graphics from a friend in ministry. This friend, Steve Fridsma, is a volunteer at an innovative church, CentrePointe, in Michigan. Steve felt empowered to begin creating his own graphics for worship. As an architect, Steve had no previous Photoshop training or experience. So instead of trying to create complex computer-based images from scratch, or use every filter in the program, Steve focused on creating simple images with single photos. The result is very effective! Your work need not be complex to be effective. My former coworker Todd Carter would say that there was an inverse law in relation to video editing: the more effects, the less effective.

J: One way to practice simplicity is to start out with on-the-street interviews (made popular by Jay Leno). All you need is a video camera, a CD player, and second VCR. Add to that someone with an outgoing personality, a good question, and an area of town where a lot of people can be questioned on camera and you're ready. It's relatively simple, and it can be very effective in worship.

#2 Develop formulas

No matter how far ahead you plan, when you face the weekly worship deadline, your skills get honed quickly. After you've spent some time developing your skills, you'll find that you also develop time-tested formulas for successful productions. I have developed standard formulas for song backgrounds, graphic backgrounds, and simple animations. These formulas are great to have in your back pocket, because some weeks you just don't have anything creative to give. At other times you are in a hurry, and don't have time to create something completely unique. In Chapter 8 you'll have the opportunity to see and produce some of those formulas that we have developed over the years.

#3 Play to your strengths

With a few successes, it's often human nature to become overconfident and attempt things well beyond our capabilities. Experimentation is a great thing, but often we should leave our experiments well hidden from the public eye. I say this as much for myself as I do for you. We have spun our wheels more times than I'd want to admit on things that were way beyond where we were at the time.

My most vivid memory of this was from one Christmas Eve service. We had spent over two years developing a style of commercial that employed a driving soundtrack and high-quality animation. That had worked so well for us that we began to think we could accomplish anything. So, we set out to create a spot that would require time-lapse photography and complicated camera equipment such as cranes, jibs, and dollys; further, to communicate the drama, we'd need to hire professional actors. After a few weeks of planning it became painfully obvious that we'd been wasting our time. We simply could not do it! We then picked up the pieces and started over with an all-animated concept.

#4 Learn your software inside and out

Knowledge of your software tool is one of the key factors in effective planning. How can you assess what's within your capabilities in a design team setting without knowing your software? If you work on a tight turnaround, you'll save yourself many headaches by digging deeply into your software when there is not a tight deadline. I know it sounds crazy, but I even read the manuals.

L: Jason and I spent many nights designing and producing in his old bachelor pad. I remember many occasions when I'd use his bathroom, and the only reading material he had was Adobe's After Effects manuals.

#5 Constantly train

Training was a constant part of my ministry at Ginghamsburg. Because of natural turnover, I continually kept ads of various styles in front of the church, recruiting new camera operators, lighting operators, and others. We had a training system in place, using people from within the ministry to teach others.

For one 6-month period while I was writing *The Wired Church*, I suspended training. After that, it took me about a year to get the ministry back to where it had been, in both size and quality of work. Perhaps the best thing a media minister can do is to constantly, I mean constantly, train.

J: But how do you get them to show up? First, serve food! It makes the difference in attracting volunteers. When food is served attendance is good. Second, mix training with fun. Spend part of the time doing hands-on training with cameras and computers, and spend the other part of the time watching recorded TV programs, such as award shows, to pick apart their live mistakes. It can be great fun.

#6 Get the best resources possible to shorten time commitments

There are some great resources out there that can greatly reduce your production time, and make your work look more professional. You can get stock video footage for everything under the sun, and still images are available on hundreds of CD-ROMs. The advantage of using stock produced material is that most of it is created by industry professionals, which means it is usually high quality. This also allows you to play to someone else's strengths.

One project called for time-lapse cloud footage. I had an old Hi-8 camera that did a poor man's version of time-lapse video, so we set it up on a tripod and sat in a field for a few hours as it recorded the sky. Later we went back and looked at the footage, and it was awful. For the next hour we played with speeding it up, slowing it down, and altering the frame rate, to no avail. We just couldn't make it work.

A company called Artbeats had three CDs full of time-lapse cloud footage. It was all shot on film, which certainly put my little RCA Hi-8 era to shame, and it was exactly what we wanted. One phone call, and $350, could have saved us hours of chasing our tails. The experience taught us an important lesson about the wisdom of looking for pre-produced resources.

#7 Stay in the culture

How do you keep your creative edge? Stay in the culture. There is a big difference between being in the culture, and being of the culture. Being in the culture means being a teachable observer. Ultimately being a student of the culture will continue to give you the edge that will keep your art fresh and relevant. Just be sure to do the work of redeeming the cultural references that you use.

When I was in art school, we had to present our instructors with reference from other sources when we designed various ads. This kept us grounded in the design trends that were current in popular culture. The same applies in the church. Researching what people are seeing at home on TV and in magazines will aid you in creating worship that relates to their daily lives.

Not a designer? That's Okay. You probably turned to experts for other tasks in your ministry, such as biblical scholarship when studying the deeper meaning of a text. Using references allows you to take advantage of the creativity and skills of professional designers everywhere. You may not be an artist, but you may be able to mimic what you see laid out in magazines and on TV. Using similar colors, fonts, and layout from an appealing magazine ad can make designing graphics for worship a cinch.

It is important to look to a variety of sources for reference, because people of all walks of life attend worship. This mean that you may find yourself thumbing through magazines you don't particularly care for, or it may mean tuning into programs and channels you don't usually watch. This is true for me. I am not a sports fan, but I often tune into ESPN to check out the latest looks, because I know many who come to church are accustomed to that look.

Look to MTV for youth imagery. The Lifetime channel appeals to women. Pay attention to the twenty-four-hour news networks (CNN, FOX, and MSNBC) for fresh graphic looks. For techno looks, check out SCI-FI Channel, and TechTV. TVLand is a great place for retro TV looks. These are just a few places to start your reference hunt.

#8 Take planned creative absences

In addition to regular time off, take time to rejuvenate your creative juices. Usually, we don't pick church conferences, but secular digital media industry conferences. Go to theme parks. At these places, we find great inspiration for our work.

#9 Watch yourself

L: One of the best ways to improve the quality of a team is through a technique learned from jazz classes. I had convinced myself that I was a darn good saxophone player. In concerts, I would stand up and scream away with my David Sanborn mouthpiece like I was really David Sanborn. Then one time I heard a recording of my performance in class. Actually witnessing myself, versus the image that I had of myself, changed my approach.

Watch yourself. Watch recordings of your worship, or get feedback from a trusted source. Critique your own work, as a team and as individuals. It's the best way to improve.

The inevitable weekend bomb

In spite of the best strategies, there will be times in the development of digital age worship that the intended experience fails miserably. This is inevitable. Sometimes when I come up with an idea for a worship video, at the moment I think of it, it is absolutely amazing. Outstanding. "A clip that will alter cinema history!" But then I start to produce it. Artists know that the creative process often takes its own course. And there have been times that when I arrive at the story's destination, I have realized that it simply doesn't work.

Unfortunately, every weekend is not worthy of a People's Choice Award. What do you do when the media piece comes up short?

Jesus had this problem once. Mark 4 tells the story of Jesus working incredibly hard at making a parable relevant and insightful in the hearts and minds of his audience. He goes to great efforts. But in spite of all his hard work, it comes up short. Both the crowd of seekers, and his cadre of followers, simply didn't get it. Sometimes a parable doesn't do its intended job, either because of production problems or audience confusion.

I have certainly had my share of production problems, both in creation and presentation. One weekend, about six months after joining a church's staff, I finally felt comfortable enough to leave the production booth. It had been my goal ever since arrival to get out of there, both as a sign of trust and empowerment to my team and because my wife was sitting alone in this big new church where we still didn't really know anyone. The teams had been performing admirably in response to their training and every week I was feeling more and more comfortable. I had complete, working crews in place, and much of my job had become sitting around with the headsets on listening to them serve.

Although most of the early stuff was a combination of live

cameras and computer stills, the team was slowly getting more comfortable integrating video playback, or "roll-ins," with our live switcher. As we started to play back video more, I began to make more original clips. One of the things that I did early on was to play back all of the pieces that I created off of the same combined "Master Reel," to avoid a generation loss copying a clip onto another tape (this was pre-nonlinear, when we were doing everything with a Hi-8 dual deck and a Sony VX-3 camera, for those of you who remember that!).

This particular weekend we had an important video to play in the middle of the pastor's sermon. It was a dramatic two-minute clip about the Promise Keepers event and how it had changed the lives of some of our local men. All weekend long the piece ran smoothly: at our Saturday 5:30 and Sunday 8:25 and 9:45 services. At the 11:00 AM time, since worship was going so well, my wife was in worship and I decided to sit with her. The service ran great, less a few minor camera hitches, and when the time came for the video roll-in during the sermon I sat confidently planted in my chair. The time came and our pastor gave the cue for the clip. The lights faded, the screen faded to black, and . . . no video. I patiently waited in my chair; sure they had just stuck it in pause. But still no video. For about 45 seconds the silence grew and the worshipful moment shrank. Then, finally, a video appeared on the screen, accompanied with the music of kids . . . singing . . . .Huh?! It was the pre-school promo from two months ago!

I leaped out of my chair in front of the sanctuary and hurried red-faced down the aisle and up to the booth. The completely inappropriate clip had been at the beginning of the current Master Reel, and the team had miscued the tape. I still remember the kids' song, playing in my head over and over like a demon jack-in-the-box. I may have been harder on myself than the congregation was on me, but in my view the preschool promo had completely ruined all the work our pastor had done in setting up the power of the Promise Keepers tape. The experience was a failure. Fortunately, the pastor's words to me after the service were healing: "Jesus is still Lord," he said. I realized that we'd move on to produce another week.

Even if your production was as all you could hope for it to be, audience confusion can still derail it. When nobody understood his parable of the sower in Mark 4, Jesus got frustrated. It's one thing for the whole crowd to not understand his point, but the disciples? The disciples were so confused they came to him privately (vv. 10-12) and wanted him to explain the whole point of using media one more time. So he did, and then said, "Aren't you ever going to get it?"

Do you ever wonder if Jesus wished he had picked different disciples? That he ever thought this poor group of dimwits was never going to be able to communicate the Word? The artist in me appreciates that sentiment. People should always be moved by my wonderful work!

Don't quit. Keep plugging away at this new thing called digital age worship. Both you and your audience will get better at it with each new production week. You'll experience weekends that fail miserably, but that doesn't mean you should fold up the screen and pack away the projector. Jesus didn't raise his screen. He took the time to teach through the failures, and at each opportunity, stepped out into the public sphere and spoke again, with the same voice and in the same style (Mark 4:21-23). Make the most of your mistakes; if it doesn't work explain the idea, even though, like a joke, explaining it is never as good as experiencing it. Then go right ahead and continue to make digital parables. And remember that Jesus is still Lord. As every teacher knows, the point of the parable is, and the greatest impact occurs, when the receiver deduces the truth on his or her own.

J: When the smoke clears, we can grow from our mistakes. One of our volunteer directors got very nervous one week, and made a series of very public mistakes in worship. The biggest of all was missing the opening call to worship, a video animation. That clip was the cue for the host to walk onto the stage, and after a few fumbles on the screen, we all realized that the clip would never come. The host, a bit shaken, had to make her way onto the stage and try to cover for the fact that something weird had just happened on-screen. It was a very awkward moment for all of us.

Immediately following the service our director came down and promptly said, "I quit." He was so disheartened by his mistakes that he thought he had destroyed worship for everyone present. We of course knew that mistakes were part of the process. Len took him aside and assured him that he would not be quitting our team. We showed him grace. The Spirit's presence was felt even in the midst of our shortcomings.

That volunteer director became one of, if not the, best director on our team. He came out on the other side stronger because of his mistakes and later went on to train others, imparting his own personal story. Our entire ministry was strengthened that day.

Chapter 8:
Digital Art Made Easy

Creating digital art is a dynamic, participatory, ongoing process. Because of that, we decided it is best to put this chapter online. Visit it at www.abingdonpress.com/ebooks. You will find a range of helpful aids for becoming digital storytellers, resources for free and inexpensive stuff, an e-mail message board for interacting with other digital story-tellers, and links to churches that are doing a great job of being digital storytellers. You can also find us on the web at www.midnightoil.net.

storm front coming

Chapter 9
Driving into the Digital Storm

L: One of our designed worship weekends is called "Storm Front Coming." Its basic premise is that conflict is an inevitable by-product of spiritual growth. Since, as the saying goes, with Jesus we find the peace that passes all understanding, it can be confusing and frustrating when following Christ creates conflict rather than peace. I know I have felt that way on many occasions, both personally and professionally. **(See "Storm Front Coming" Chapter 26 on the DVD.)**

"Storm Front Coming" is an experience for people to find comfort in the experience that following Christ is not all blue sky, whether in relation to contemporary worship, family attitudes toward your faith, or personal faith development. In each step of faith, Jesus is our sustaining force. It is based on Luke 12:49-56, where Jesus declares that following him will turn people against their own family, whether that might mean their actual family or their spiritual family.

You may be feeling the anxiousness of looming conflict in your own personal or spiritual family after having read this book. God's calling to become digital storytellers includes the need to deal with the inevitable conflict that will arise from those who resist based on whatever reason, be it a conserving attitude about the tradition, a rejection of culture, or confusion about the source of their faith. Veterans of the working world know that there is no utopian environment; the constant dynamic of people coming and going requires an ongoing process of managing the storms that come from pursuing a vision. Take comfort in knowing that such resistance is actually a sign that you're doing something important. Of course, it's impossible to make everyone happy, or to build the perfect sandbag barriers against the coming storm. To conquer storms, you've sometimes got to drive straight into the eye, like the team in the film Twister. Staying in the safe religious places of the old culture, now passing away, doesn't require much risk, or a lot of faith. It's essential that we go into the dangerous places in order to truly experience renewal, and deepen our discipleship.

Overcoming fears

Driving into the storm means confronting our fears. These fears are numerous. For example, church leaders often have fears that digital age worship might dilute conversations that have been rhetorical and didactic, that challenge people to a deeper faith commitment. As an advocate, I recognize the need for this sort of in-depth study. I remember being frustrated for many years in not being able to find a group of people with whom to have a regular intelligent Bible study. If we think that this type of discipleship is open to erasure, we misunderstand the parameters of digital culture. As explained in Chapter 2, digital culture does not mark the end of rational, abstract thinking; it reforms it with new circuitry: one in which worship works alongside small groups for education and discipleship, even for "seekers," rather than replacing it.

A second fear church leaders have is that they might misrepresent or misinterpret the Gospel. Many leaders will read books like this one and be saturated with knowledge about a subject, but never actually go out and DO anything. Fear drives their frozen state; they say, "I want to make sure I'm doing it right," and they never do anything at all.

J: What you already know about planning worship will

still work. The exegetical process is very similar to what you learned from biblical scholars in seminary. Biblical literacy employs methods similar to media literacy.

L: Should digital worship planners have a thoughtful, prayerful eye about their work for worship? Of course! Should they not do something for fear that it won't be pure or sacred enough for God? Of course not. Trust that God will work through such an imperfect vessel as you, or as the people with whom you create.

One of the best things about media ministry is the freedom that we give each other as worship planners to experiment in what we often call our "living laboratory." Some weekends are horrible, both early on and even later, when we become "experts." But, some weekends will be incredible, too. Just like some sermons.

A third fear is the resistant congregation. People don't fear change, they fear being changed. They fear the loss of control. They fear being cast into a murky environment without being able to trust in strong leadership to lead them through. This is leadership to whom they can give their trust, and leadership that responds to their own concerns and ideas. People respond best when they are allowed to discover God's truth, not when they are coerced into signing metaphorical statements of belief. The role of the leader is to influence thinking.

A church in Oregon that worshiped with approximately five hundred per weekend introduced media for the first time in a simple manner. They set up TVs on carts around their sanctuary, all of which were fed a signal from a VCR that sat under the pulpit. The screens remained black for all of worship, save one clip from a movie that the pastor used during the sermon. After that weekend, no TVs were present in worship for the next six weeks, so the furor could die down. Then, the TVs came back. Second absence was four weeks. Then a third time. Eventually, people from the congregation began to come to the pastor and say, "Hey, those clips are pretty neat! Why don't you do that more often?" All of a sudden, the presence of media in worship became a grassroots movement rather than a top-down mandate. The leadership of that church had demonstrated its value, and generated a level of excitement that wanted more, rather than forcing it on the congregation.

Passion overcomes fear. Find team members for whom fear is not a driving force, the sort of people who will dive into a new computer application because they want to accomplish an idea, rather than waiting for the six-week training class at the community college. Give examples of what transformational digital art looks, feels, and sounds like through your interaction with them. Support their ideas as you lead with your own. Enable them to find purpose in their work. Purpose and passion are the complementary colors of the image of leadership. Deep compassion for people is the sustaining passion for ministry of any type, whether it is hospice care or digital age worship. Properly focused, passion marries with hope to give people the courage to lead into new expressions of ministry.

J: A fourth fear is the financial undertaking that this requires. This fear is really based in the unknown. Computer and projection equipment have come down in price so much that this can be done for less than half of what it cost just three years ago. If you can siphon a small portion of that organ restoration fund, you can start a media ministry! Up front, you might need to rent or borrow to demonstrate the need, but it you do it well, folks will come out of the woodwork to make it happen. When you begin to show how this new worship form is changing lives, people will want to support it.

At one point late in a conference at a small church in Texas I shared that you can begin to create digital age worship for $75 a quarter. A man came to me immediately after we finished, and said that he had spent most of the day inspired but distracted by the cost he thought was associated with doing digital age worship. He said, "You should share your costs at the very beginning, because most of us fear that the cost will be too great for our limited church budgets."

L: Whether it's our resources or some of the many other possibilities listed on the web site mentioned in Chapter 8, an entire industry for supporting digital age worship is forming. Increasingly, cost is no longer prohibitive to even the smallest churches.

The heart of a digital storyteller

Managing change is a vital part of becoming a digital storyteller. There have always been those in life who like change, and those who don't. The book *The Future and Its Enemies* put labels on these two types of people: dynamists and stasists.[53] Are you by nature a dynamist, or a change-oriented person? The work of producing digital age worship is by nature an act of moving forward. We are all agents of change for a church often controlled by stasists, or reactionary control freaks insistent on the status quo, who are most comfortable with the way it's always been done.

A colleague once kept an old advertisement on his office wall that showed a rumpled pair of men's briefs with the words above it, "Change Is Good." Continued resistance to media within the walls of progressive churches often surprises people. Why does every church repeatedly fight the same battles? There are many reasons for this resistance, among them: new families unaware of the past, a continual struggle to create artistic expressions of media for worship and education, and the natural tendency for people to confuse Jesus with the horse he rode into their lives.

Churched people don't start out as stasists. They simply find expressions for their faith in a particular culture, or time and place. Not challenged to move beyond that culture, they over time confuse their experience of Jesus with the cultural context of that experience. Eventually, they come to believe that certain songs or ways of worship are more sacred than others are, and that to change them would be sacrilege.

Jesus' rant recorded in Matthew 23 (the "seven woes") is against people who have forgotten the meaning behind their activity, and have put ritual ahead of real faith. Thank God that Jesus is capable of reaching beyond these barriers, now as well as then. Being a media producer in a church is the perfect opportunity to strip away the confusion. A new medium gives us an opportunity to speak the Gospel message in fresh ways, not to merely repeat meaningless ritual.

The famous Scopes monkey trial of the 1920s was one of the first media-frenzied trials with which we have since become so familiar. But the abstract issue of creation versus evolution was only the top layer of a deeply symbolic event. Modern life, with its scientific method, was becoming culturally dominant, and it sharply contrasted with the agricultural heritage that many people still lived. Reason started interfering with many comfortable theologies. What the creationists at the trial were really calling for was a return to a time of simpler faith and values, without the issues and problems of modern life.

Change is inevitable. What we must do as followers of the great change agent, Jesus, is to struggle in the wake of change and find how we reconcile our core, unchanging beliefs with the constantly changing cultural forms of the world. The lazy or comfortable nature in each of us cannot blame critics of digital age worship. It would be a lot easier to go back to the good old ways of doing religion. Established models require less work in any field of society or personal protocol. But that is not what we are taught active faith is about.

A sign posted outside of an art gallery read, "Art is a sign of life. There can be no life without change, as there can be no development without change. To be afraid of what is different is to be afraid of life." Not a notice for a controversial new exhibit, this sign was outside a New York Museum of Modern Art exhibit featuring Picasso and Matisse. The year: 1912.[54]

Embracing new cultural forms keeps our faith fresh. It makes us vital, useful workers for God's kingdom. It enables us to once again see the simple truth that formed our initial transformations in Christ as we see others, through their own languages, experiencing the same things. And, perhaps most important, it puts us in the same category as the original Gospel advocate, John the Baptist, who preached radical change. Abandoning the altar as the means to God (what complete heresy!), John preached baptism and the cleansing of sins, for the purpose of making way for the coming Kingdom of God. Change, for John, served a very specific purpose—it cleared away the obstacles so that people could experience Jesus.

Take a minute and think of what communication forms you used this past Sunday in your worship. How does what you did create an experience of the Gospel for digital culture? Although certainly valid and needed, don't limit your work in media ministry to just doing what is known as IMAG (image magnification), or support for sermons and group singing. Realize that what you are dealing with is an entirely new communication system. Understanding this new communication system has been the goal of this book.

J: By now you have begun to think about your own heart as a digital storyteller. Ultimately you will form your own vision, but let's review just a few key points:

- When designing digital age worship, education and inspiration become fused together with experiences rooted in story, and communicated through digital art.
- A narrative approach to worship gives a holistic picture of the Gospel, which goes beyond a lesson-of-the-day mentality that focuses on behavior modification, to a deeper understanding of who we are in Christ.
- Stay committed to creating art that relates to the "average" person in worship.
- Discard old definitions for worship. Focus on authenticity.
- Forming and articulating your vision is of extreme importance. Sticking to that vision through the storm is a must for growth to happen.
- Mistakes are inevitable! Keep your chin up, learn from it, and keep moving forward.
- And finally, digital age worship is not about technology, it's about culture.

L: Create and incorporate digital art that dares to speak the Gospel through its own innate characteristics by engaging an experience in the receiver. Embrace the integration of media into church life. Practice change. Becoming a digital dynamist means that the call of God is ever present. Life in Jesus is about change, about turning around, and good digital art reflects that life. In all you do, have courage. The end of that art exhibit sign in 1912 said that the exhibit was a proclamation "against cowardice." A radical digital dynamist himself, Jesus is our courage giver, empowering us to be creators for worship in the digital age. So, drive straight into whatever storm is on your windshield.

J: The good news is that we don't have to weather the storms alone. You may fear becoming lost in this new wilderness, where everything seems beyond your capabilities. So we'd like to share another recent experience we've designed. It is called the Wilderness Guide. This story may give you hope for the upcoming storms that will come as you walk through uncharted territory. Read the words of Jesus (and **Experience "The Wilderness Guide," Chapter 29 on the DVD.**):

> I still have many things to tell you, but you cannot handle them now. But when the Spirit of Truth comes he will take you by the hand, and guide you into all the truth there is. He won't draw attention to himself, but will make sense out of what is about to happen. And indeed out of all I have done and said He will honor me. He will take from me and deliver it to you. All that belongs to the Father is mine. That is why I have said the Spirit takes from me and delivers to you. (John 16:12-15)

In 1804, Lewis and Clark explored the American wilderness long before there were maps or roads or signs to tell them what direction to go. A pregnant, fifteen-year-old Native American named Sacagawea became their interpreter and guide across thousands of miles of uncharted territory. She gave them true direction; she was a reliable counselor. Like the disciples in the story, we all tend to operate out of a fear of abandonment and rejection, particularly in times of transition. Jesus gives us the guidance of the Holy Spirit to help us manage through the wildernesses of our digital future.

The Spirit Guide will not leave you. There are obstacles on the path, trails that are misleading, and animals that prey on your very existence as you try to settle this new land, but take heart, if you follow the Wilderness Guide, your journey will be successful. When you feel weak remember Christ's words: "He will take from me and deliver it to you." Do not be swayed by the feeling of loneliness that comes with being a pioneer. The Holy Spirit will be with you, and as you establish the path, others will join you. Lives will be changed because you have chosen to walk this path.

May you have the courage of Christ to dare define the art of ministry in a digital culture.

---

53. Virginia Postrel, *The Future and Its Enemies: The Growing Conflict Over Creativity, Enterprise, and Progress* (New York: The Free Press, 1998).
54. Jennings, p. 44.

Appendix
An
Annotated Mediography

L: There are so many ideas that impinge on art and the church in digital culture that I could not begin to reference any sort of exhaustive list. Instead, in all humility, I have provided just a few references that shed some light on digital storytelling for me:

1. Babin, Pierre. *The New Era in Religious Communication.* Minneapolis: Fortress, 1991.
   A scholarly overview on Christian communication, with specific emphasis on education and Catholic communities. Babin was talking about the "quest for religious experience" ten years ago.

2. Bennis, Warren. *Organizing Genius: The Secrets of Creative Collaboration.* Addison Wesley, 1997.
   An excellent series of case studies of various teams that did incredible things (e.g., the team that made the Macintosh). Best book on teams, from a secular perspective.

3. Boomershine, Thomas. *Story Journey.* Nashville: Abingdon, 1988.
   Tom's emphasis on the power of a narrative approach to the Bible has been way ahead of its time. His book gives a few examples of such power in his own life.

4. Cordeiro, Wayne. *Doing Church as a Team: Launching Effective Ministries Through Teamwork.* Gospel Light, 1998.
   A pastor's strategies for forming a wildly fruitful team-based church. Best book on teams, from a Christian perspective.

5. Eisenstein, Elizabeth. *The Printing Press as an Agent of Change.*

The standard text on radical changes in technology in another time.

6. Field, Syd. *Screenplay: The Foundations of Screenwriting.* New York: Dell, 1994.

   Now in its third edition, this is the classic for making Hollywood stories. Its value lies in its approach to the story structure, which has been a formative part of my approach to worship.

7. Ford, Kevin Graham. *Jesus for a New Generation: Putting the Gospel in the Language of Xers.* Downers Grove, Ill: InterVarsity Press, 1995.

   Great narrative-form review of the mind-sets of the postmodern generation from the grandson of Billy Graham.

8. Giannetti, Louis. *Understanding Movies, 8th ed.* Prentice Hall, ISBN 0136465633.

   As mentioned, a standard text on film.

9. Gloman, Chuck B. and Tom LeTourneau. *Placing Shadows: Lighting Techniques for Video Production.* Boston: Focal Press, 2000.

   The basic difference between professional and amateur video is lighting and shadows, not the camera's brand and format. This book is a great primer on the use of lighting in digital video production.

10. Lewis, C. S. *God in the Dock.* Grand Rapids: Eerdmans, 1994.

    From one who understood the relationship of church and culture well.

11. Morgenthaler, Sally. *Worship Evangelism.* Grand Rapids: Zondervan, 1999.

    Nails the basic issue of keeping a focus on the immanent presence of our transcendent God in worship so well that you'd think everybody believes the same way. The best primer for worship in digital culture I've read.

12. Negroponte, Nicholas. *Being Digital*. New York: Alfred A. Knopf, 1995.
    A visionary book about the future direction of personal computers, and to a large degree, about society by extension.

13. Neibuhr, H. Richard. *Christ and Culture*. Harper-Collins, 1986.
    The classic study on the relationships of Christians to culture, originally published in 1951. Articulates a basic ministry typology that still holds true in many ways.

14. Postrel, Virginia. *The Future and Its Enemies: The Growing Conflict Over Creativity, Enterprise, and Progress*. New York: The Free Press, 1998.
    A fabulous restructuring of traditional political boundaries (left/right) into a new rubric of chicken littles versus annies. Postrel believes in the living lab approach to life, "human betterment," comes from trial and error, not from prewritten scripts of the future.

15. Sample, Tex. <u>*The Spectacle of Worship in a Wired World: Electronic Culture and the Gathered People of God.*</u> Nashville: Abingdon, 1998.
    Sample is a scholar who embraces the theory of digital culture. This book is ideally useful for giving language to moderns, to speak to other moderns, about digital culture.

16. Schmitt, Bernd. *Experiential Marketing: How to Get Customers to Sense, Feel, Think, Act and Relate to Your Company and Brands*. New York: The Free Press, 1999.
    See Chapter 2.

17. Slaughter, Michael, *Out on the Edge: A Wake-Up Call for Church Leaders on the Edge of the Media Reformation*. Nashville: Abingdon, 1998.
    The book that formed from our early design team experiments in digital age worship and that were

capsulated in the "Media Reformation" one-day conference Mike and I did.

18. Sweet, Leonard I. *Soul Tsunami: Sink or Swim in New Millennium Culture*. Grand Rapids: Zondervan, 1999.
    A postmodern ministry primer for pastors. For a more detailed framework of Sweet, read his earlier work, *Faithquakes*, Nashville: Abingdon, 1994.

19. ———. *Post-Modern Pilgrims: First Century Passion for the 21st Century Church*. Nashville: Broadman and Holman, 2001.
    More thoughts on the same basic subject.

20. ———, ed. *Communication and Change in American Religious History*. Grand Rapids: Eerdmans, 1993.
    A series of essays that explore the relationships of ministry and communication systems in American history.

21. Tapscott, Don. *Growing Up Digital*
    An excellent analysis of digital culture.

22. White, Susan, *Christian Worship and Technological Change*. Nashville: Abingdon, 1994.
    In a period where "technology" means new technology, this book reminds the reader that, among other things, every artifact used to communicate the Word is technology, whether it is a pencil or a projector.

23. Wilson, Len. *The Wired Church: Making Media Ministry*. Nashville: Abingdon, 1999.
    The Wired Church is for local church media ministries, but is also the first step toward outlining a digital media ministry approach that is equal parts theory and practice.